Living Freedom

LOSING A SPIRITUAL 10 LBS.

Alison Wallwork

xulon
PRESS

Endorsements

Alison's words are conversational, warm, vulnerable and caring. After a few paragraphs you will feel as if she were an old friend. Her testimony is inspiring, struggles relatable, and her love for Jesus oozes out of every sentence.

–Jenna Lucado Bishop

Author, *Love Is...Six Lessons On What Love Looks Like; From Blah to Awe: Shaking Up a Boring Faith*

National Speaker, Revolve Tour

Living Freedom: Losing a Spiritual 10 lbs. is a must read for women of ALL ages. It is filled with practical truths as well as refreshingly honest personal experiences. Using stories from her own life and the lives of others she has encountered, Alison is able to help shed light on the issues holding so many women back today. You will be challenged, inspired, and moved to action as you read through the pages of this book!

–Pastor Tommy Barnett

Senior Pastor, Phoenix First Assembly

Author, *The Power of a Half Hour*

The journey to uncovering buried pain can seem like an uninvited interruption, yet completely necessary if one is to laugh easily and love life. I got caught up in *Living Freedom: Losing a Spiritual 10 lbs.* as Alison uses real-life stories to help us learn to embrace God's complete healing for our past wounds and disarm the lodged memories that hold us captive. This book is an engaging resource for women who truly desire to live out our true limitless heritage as daughters of the King!

–Audrey Meisner

Bestselling Author, *Marriage Under Cover*

TV Host, *My New Day*

Alison has a refreshing way to express how to live free. This is a powerful yet practical way to focus on living a spiritually and physically free life. A great read on how to overcome.

–David Friend

Senior Pastor, North Scottsdale Christian

Author, *Freedom in Your Finances*

Sharing from her own painful experience, Alison transparently reveals her journey from bondage to freedom. If you find yourself encumbered by a heavy load that God has not intended you to carry, Alison Wallwork's book, *Living Freedom: Losing a Spiritual 10 lbs.* is a must read. She beautifully unfolds God's plan and desire for you to "shed the weight" that loads you down.

–Rev. Dawn Scott Jones

Author, *When A Woman You Love Was Abused: A Husband's Guide to Helping Her Overcome Childhood Sexual Molestation*

National Speaker

Table of Contents

Acknowledgements xi

Introduction xiii

Section 1: Identifying Your Problem Areas

Chapter 1   The Battle of the Bulge 21

Chapter 2   Fear & Insecurity 28

Chapter 3   Old Wounds.. 46

Chapter 4   Complacency... 66

Chapter 5   Misconceptions 75

Section 2: Losing the Weight

Chapter 6   The Power of Peace & Joy 95

Chapter 7   Strut Your Stuff 112

Chapter 8   Living Loved.. 123

Section 3: Keeping it Off!

Chapter 9   Daily Choices... 139

Chapter 10   Contagious Freedom 152

Acknowledgements

───────── ⌘ ─────────

To my amazing husband, thank you for believing in me. Thank you for loving me and for pursuing my heart. God gave me more than I ever dared hope for when He gave you to me, and I'm eternally grateful.

To Malaki, Zayne, Mataio, and soon coming baby boy # 4, I am grateful every day for the privilege of being your mom! Thank you for the nights when you would pray for my book during your bedtime prayers, even though "it's boring because there are no pictures." Thank you for keeping our lives exciting and full of life and love. My prayer is that you will catch onto God's love and freedom way earlier than I did.

To my mom, thanks for always praying for me and for all your hard work as a single mom.

To my mother-in-law, thank you for the many times you took the older boys so I could write while the baby slept.

Thanks for all your prayers as well. And thank you for raising such an incredible man with whom I get to do life!

To Debbie, thank you for reading this chapter by chapter as I was writing and being my encourager along the way. You have been an incredible mentor, and I am so grateful for the way you love my family.

To Junior, thank you for being a spiritual father and mentor to me when I most needed one. You taught me how to open my heart to my Heavenly Father, and you've never stopped propelling me forward.

To Steve and Jen who gave writing advice along the way and read many revisions, I greatly appreciate your time, thoughts, and involvement.

To Diane Kulkarni, thank you for the hours you put into editing my work. You were an answer to prayer.

To all my leaders and mentors along the way who poured God's love and truth into my life, thank you! To list all of you would take a chapter in itself! You helped me learn so much about letting go and letting God in. You pushed me out of my comfort zone and prayed me through many tough seasons. Some of you have loved me like family, and some of you have become great friends. I'm thankful for all of you.

Introduction

I accepted Jesus into my heart as a young child, but it wasn't until I was an adult that I began understanding there was freedom that I could have in Christ. I believed that I had been saved from hell, and I knew there were certain things I should and shouldn't do if I was going to call myself a Christian. I experienced the presence of God several times in my life, saw Him answer prayers, and heard Him speak to my heart. Yet I was still walking around bound by so many unresolved issues. My dad's suicide and the inescapable effects it had on my life were at the top of that list. I allowed shame, anger, insecurity, and doubt (just to name a few) to stay in my heart, and as a result, I became bound by them. Instead of running to God for healing, I ran from Him. I was confused, empty, burdened, desperate, and sure that I did not want to keep living my life so weighed down.

So let God work his will in you. Yell a loud no to the Devil and watch him scamper. Say a quiet yes to God and he'll be there in no time. Quit dabbling in sin. Purify your inner life. Quit playing the field. Hit bottom, and cry your eyes out. The fun and games are over. Get serious, really serious. Get down on your knees before the Master; it's the only way you'll get on your feet. James 4:7-10 (The Message)

I discovered the truth of this verse in my own life. I began to seek God, and I have never been the same. The realization that there is true freedom in Christ started a new journey for me. It's one that I've been on ever since, and it involves making choices that help me live in that freedom every day.

I'm not claiming to be an expert. There are definitely days when I still try to take on things that I need to give to God instead. My relationship with God is a journey just like yours. I'm constantly still learning and growing, but I have definitely realized *how* to let go of the burdens that can easily weigh me down. I've learned how to get rid of my excess spiritual baggage, and I can honestly say that *most* days, I walk in that.

Freedom is *meant* to be lived! God created us to be women who walk around living free, yet few truly do. In this book, I am going to address some common problem areas that typically hold us back so that we can discover the tools we need to fight for our freedom, hold onto it, live it, and give it away to others. This is definitely not an overnight process, nor is it something that just happens. We must choose to be deliberate about it.

Maybe you're someone who is carrying around years of baggage, and you're not sure how to get rid of it. Maybe there are things that have happened in your life that you have never dealt with. Maybe your heart is heavy and joy isn't a part of your daily life. Maybe you walk around feeling uncomfortable in your own skin. Whatever burden you're bearing, this book is for you.

Physical training is good, but training for godliness is much better, promising benefits in this life and in the life to come. 1 Timothy 4:8

Many women become obsessed with improving their physical appearance. Most women would love to quickly lose five or ten pounds. I searched the word "diets" on the internet just to see how many sites would come up. I was shocked to see over 22,800,000 different websites popping up in less than a second! I'm sure that number will continue to increase as time goes on. I also read an article online that said the average woman spends *31 years* of her life dieting.[1]

Wow! We can get so focused on our outward appearance that we neglect to work on what's going on inside of us. I'm all for being healthy and improving our bodies when needed or wanted, but according to 1 Timothy 4:8, focusing on our spiritual health benefits us far more.

Dealing with our spiritual state is similar to dealing with our physical appearance. It takes work, discipline, and determination, but the outcome is worth it! When our spiritual life is strong, we are better able to handle the challenges life brings. That's why I wrote this book. It is possible to shed the unnecessary burdens in life that steal our freedom. Jesus has promised us an abundant life, and we *can* live in it!

Strip down, start running—and never quit! No extra spiritual fat, no parasitic sins. Keep your eyes on Jesus, who both began and finished this race we're in. Study how he did it. Because he never lost sight of where he was headed— that exhilarating finish in and with God. Hebrews 12:1-3 (The Message)

It's hard to run when you're carrying extra weight around. I don't typically advise stripping, but in this case, we have a race to finish, so get ready to strip down!

Many of you may have "known" God for years, your whole life even, and still have not grasped that you truly are free in Christ! That was my story. In several of the chapters ahead, you'll come across seven different stories from other women who have also battled hard things, some of which you may have faced or are currently facing. These sections are simply called "She's Living Freedom" because that's exactly what they are now doing. As you read this book, my hope is that you will begin to drop some of that excess weight you've been carrying around, and walk away feeling lighter, refreshed, and ready to start living freedom!

Section 1

Identifying Your Problem Areas

CHAPTER 1

The Battle of the Bulge

I will gladly admit that I would never stand on a scale to weigh myself holding onto *anything* extra. Usually I'm trying to find anything and everything that can be taken off before stepping on the scale...shoes, sunglasses, belt, jacket, purse, accessories. I prefer to stand on the scale naked, but that really only works in my own home! I would venture to say there are other women out there who feel the same way.

As women, most of us have that frustrating, stubborn area on our bodies that seems to gain weight so quickly but takes so long to get rid of, such as the stomach, arms, thighs, hips, etc. We know we *want* to get rid of the fat. We may even know *how* to get rid of it. But actually slimming down is an entirely different thing!

Have you ever stopped to think of the spiritual trouble spots in your life that are like that as well, such as anger, bitterness, rejection, unforgiveness, disappointment, stress, shame, offense, or insecurity? If we are truly honest with ourselves, we often hold onto excess weight in the spiritual realm that we need to get rid of. We even burden ourselves down with extra duties and activities we add to our schedules in the effort to be more. One of the biggest "bulges" we face as women is the feeling that we are not good enough. We get this sense that we don't measure up to the bar that we want to measure up to, so we try harder and take on more. This in turn usually leaves us frustrated and emotionally drained. We're dragging around extra baggage everywhere we go! As a result, we are worn out, overwhelmed, stressed, discouraged, TIRED, and definitely not free. This is exactly where the enemy would like to keep us: trapped, defeated, and ready to give up.

If we want to get to a place where we are truly confident and comfortable in our own skin and in our own lives, then we have to first reach that place inside. So, instead of looking at what else we can pick up, over the next few chapters, we are going to look at *getting rid* of some of that extra weight we carry around in our spiritual lives!

Let's start by getting some help from the Expert, our Creator, who breathed and inspired His Word into account. *It is for freedom that Christ has set us free.* Galatians 5:1 (NIV)

The dictionary defines freedom as, "exemption from constraint or control" and "liberty of choice or action."

The Message paraphrase says Galatians 5:1 this way, *Christ has set you free to live a free life. So take your stand! Never again let anyone put a harness of slavery on you.* I love the way *The Message* explains things, but I almost wonder why that verse *needs* to be explained? Imagine someone in jail, or bound by handcuffs or chains for any amount of time. You wouldn't think that you would need to tell a prisoner what to do once she is free. You would think that she would have been already dreaming, hoping for, and planning that moment of deliverance and the moments thereafter. You shouldn't need to warn that newly freed soul not to pick those chains back up again, but there it is in the Bible, so there must be a reason.

You see the Bible makes it clear that there is a battle going on right now for our freedom. John 10:10 (NKJV) records Jesus saying, *The thief does not come except to steal, kill, and to destroy. I have come that they may have life, and that they may have it more abundantly."* Jesus came to give life. Satan comes to steal that life, to destroy it. Those are opposing forces. One *will* beat out the other. Jesus guarantees us victory with Him, but it is up to us to *choose* to follow His ways.

We are given the choice to walk in life or death everyday. Will we choose the blessings God has for us? Deuteronomy 30:19-20 says, *Today I have given you the choice between life and death, between blessings and curses. Now I call on heaven and earth to witness the choice you make. Oh, that you would choose life, so that you and your descendants might live! You can make this choice by loving the LORD your God, obeying him, and committing yourself firmly to him. This is the key to your life. And if you love and obey the LORD, you will live long in the land the LORD swore to give your ancestors Abraham, Isaac, and Jacob.*

The Father wants us to choose life, but He won't make us. It sounds so easy when it is presented like that, doesn't it? If, before you left your house in the morning, you had two front doors to pick from, one labeled "life" and the other "death," it would be easy to choose life. You would probably make the right choice every day!

It doesn't happen that way though. Our choice typically happens in a much quieter, more subtle way in our minds and is then carried out into our actions. So how do we consciously make the right decision when it's *not* easy? How do we battle and get rid of those stubborn, nagging thoughts that seem so overwhelming when our world is spinning out of control and our circumstances seem insurmountable? How *do* we choose life, and what does that look like in our everyday lives?

Deliverance comes when we determine to do what we are instructed while keeping our eyes (and faith) on Jesus, like Hebrews 12:1-3 says. We must continue moving forward with Him. Get rid of the stuff in your life that is holding you back from being all God has called you to be! My prayer, dear sister, is that the desire for freedom is beginning to rise up in your spirit! We are not helpless in this battle. There is victory to be gained and freedom to be lived. Let's fight the battle of the bulge in our spiritual lives and uncover some common "problem areas" many of us face. Let's begin to shed this weight, so we can run our race and live the life we were created for! Before we dive in let's spend a few moments with the Father.

Let's pray:

Father, You know exactly where I am right now in my life. I need Your freedom! I want Your freedom! I've been living without it long enough now, and I ask that You would lead me as I take this journey with You towards the things You have for me. I pray that Your Holy Spirit would reveal to me the areas in my life that have been holding me back. I also pray for the strength and the grace to lay those things down. I eagerly anticipate the outcome, and I look forward to standing on the other side of this mountain. I love You Father with all that I am. I will follow as You lead. In Jesus' Name, Amen.

Chapter 1 Reflection

As you start the process toward living freedom, write down the problem areas the Holy Spirit shows you so you can begin to deal with them and overcome them.

_____

_____

_____

_____

_____

_____

_____

_____

_____

_____

CHAPTER 2

Fear & Insecurity

*I*t was our first year of marriage. My husband, Aryan, and I were directors in a large, full-time, young adult discipleship ministry, and I was feeling very overwhelmed! Sitting on the floor of our living room one night, I began whining to God about all my insecurities. I asked Him why I always felt so unsure of myself and sought Him to take those feelings away. In the midst of my complaining, I distinctly felt Him lead me to go to Ephesians 6:10-18. I pulled out my Bible and opened it to that familiar passage. I had memorized that section before, so I was reading it and thinking "Okay. it's the armor of God passage. There's nothing in here about insecurity!"

I read it again, and this time I heard the Lord ask me, *"Why would I give you armor if I never intended you to use it?"* At that moment, the answer became obvious: **while I had been asking Him to take away my insecurity, He reminded me that He had already given me the armor and the weapons to defeat it!** He also lovingly and directly spoke to my spirit that night and said, "When you allow your insecurities to hold you back from doing what I've called you to do, it becomes *disobedience*."

Now this statement left me a little shocked. I remember thinking, "God, that's kind of harsh isn't it? I mean everyone has insecurities." Yet, it's so true! The Lord began to show me that although all people struggle with insecurities, we often just let them become an excuse, and when we allow them to stop us from doing what God has called us to do, it *is* a big deal! I had used this excuse too many times in my life, but I realized that I didn't want to miss out on God's plan for me any longer.

Now several years later, I love to ask a room full of women this question, "How many of us have ever felt insecure?" The response is always the same. There is not a hand in the room that doesn't go up! I have yet to meet a woman who never feels unsure of herself.

We ALL face this timidity at times, yet we try so hard to cover it up. We pack layer after layer on top of it, desperately trying to portray a flawless impression. But does that strategy work? No! The reason it doesn't work is because freedom doesn't come from putting more and more layers *on*! It comes from allowing those layers to be taken *off* by surrendering to the truth of God's Word.

Insecurity wreaks havoc on our emotions. It causes us to feel ashamed, guilty, worthless, unloved, degraded, and unacceptable. We feel like nothing we do is good enough because *we* are unworthy, and so we believe that we are tainted and alone. This is a lie Satan uses to weigh us down and keep us in bondage! If we let these emotions entangle us, they will choke out the life that God has given us, causing us to either pull away from those we love, or attack them, so they will not have the opportunity to hurt us. Neither of these extremes is how God intended us to live. In fact, if we continually use these approaches in our relationships, they will be destroyed.

The enemy makes us feel like we are not beautiful, secure, or accepted, the core longings of a woman's heart. They are in our make-up (and I don't mean the kind we put on)! They are just part of who we are. God created those desires in us. Because of this, the enemy relentlessly attacks us in those areas. How? He does it by distorting the way we view ourselves, others, and even God.

Let's ask ourselves these questions: What makes us feel confident? What do we find beautiful? Our answers to these questions will reveal a lot about where our security lies. If we find it centers in temporal things like appearance, relationships, or people's praise, it won't be consistent and we'll wear ourselves out constantly seeking more.

Quite a bit of our insecurity as women comes from comparing ourselves to others. This is so dangerous because it always leads to lies. We jump to wrong conclusions about others and ourselves and end up right where the enemy wants us! If we can keep looking at other people to determine our value, we'll never fully realize it because our true worth can only come from God.

True security and confidence are the fruit of our relationship with God, and that assurance is beautiful. It shows that we know who we are, and we're not looking to anyone or anything else to define us. Our certainty doesn't come from being flawless or perfect; if that were true, none of us could ever have it. The sooner we realize and believe that God finds us beautiful, precious, and worth loving, the sooner we can begin walking in freedom!

We *all* long to be secure. God longs for that for us as well. As a parent, it would break my heart if my children thought they were worthless! I would hate to see them walking around with their heads down always feeling unworthy and rejected. I bet that's how God must feel. We are His girls! He created us. He sees our worth. How must He feel when we minimize all He has given us?

The Root Problem

Fear is at the root of all of our insecurity. We fear failure, rejection, the unknown, losing control, the future, what others think, abandonment, not being good enough, etc. Worry over our fears takes on many different forms, but fear has the same root, and it produces the same result: bondage! *For God has not given us a spirit of fear and timidity, but of power, love and self-discipline.* 2 Timothy 1:7

Fear is not from God! It prevents us from enjoying an abundant life of opportunities. If we allow it to, this dread will immobilize us, halt our growth, and keep us from walking in God's power. As a result of yielding to fear, we build walls of defense, and once those walls are built, the enemy keeps them securely in place. Satan seeks to eliminate God's wisdom by twisting our perception of Him. Fear can be very powerful, but it is only has power over us if we succumb to it!

Recognition in Our Own Lives

I enjoy watching NBC's "The Biggest Loser." I love to see the transformation take place in the lives of the contestants. I get to watch them take this amazing journey to become the person they really want to be. A lot of their effort, of course, has to do with improving their physical appearance, but anyone who watches the show also knows that the trainers are always pushing them to figure out why they are carrying around so much weight. Some of the contestants know why they struggle with their weight, while others have to reach a breaking point before they realize the events that have led them down the road they are on. Regardless of what they find, the issue is that they must acknowledge it. If they don't, once the show is over, they will generally revert back to their former behavior.

This same concept is true in our spiritual lives as well. We have to take a spiritual assessment of ourselves and figure out why we are acting and reacting a certain way. Do our choices reflect bondage or freedom? If bondage, it's time to figure out where our focus is. The only way to overcome is by focusing on God. If we look at ourselves, we are only as secure as we *feel*. If we place it on other people, we are only as secure as they make us feel. Both of these ways leave us overwhelmed and heavy!

It's a Feeling

At times women's emotions can be all over the place! This is especially true when we are pregnant, going through PMS, menopause, raising toddlers *or* teenagers, undergoing major changes, or just because we "feel" like it! Hormones play a part in this, but also by nature, women tend to be more emotional. Because of this, we can easily react from emotions, which is usually not good thing!

We should remember that insecurity is an emotion. That doesn't mean it's not powerful, but as children of God, it's not who we were created to be. Yes, most of us are fearful at times, but we have been created for victory. However, we cannot succeed if we are paralyzed by fear and insecurity!

What the Word Says

But you belong to God, my dear children. You have already won a victory…because the Spirit who lives in you is greater than the spirit who lives in the world. 1 John 4:4

God is our refuge and strength, always ready to help in times of trouble. So we will not fear when earthquakes come and when the mountains crumble into the sea. Psalm 46:1-2

He will cover you with his feathers. He will shelter you with his wings. His faithful promises are your armor and protection. Do not be afraid of the terrors of the night, nor the arrow that flies in the day. Do not dread the disease that stalks in the darkness, nor the disaster that strikes at midday. Psalm 91:4-6

Surely the righteous will never be shaken; they will be remembered forever. They will have no fear of bad news; their hearts are steadfast, trusting in the LORD. Their hearts are secure, they will have no fear; in the end they will look in triumph on their foes. Psalm 112:6-8 (NIV)

When you lie down, you will not be afraid; when you lie down, your sleep will be sweet. Have no fear of sudden disaster or of the ruin that overtakes the wicked, for the LORD will be your confidence and will keep your foot from being snared. Proverbs 3:24-26 (NIV)

Fear of man will prove to be a snare, but whoever trusts in the LORD is kept safe. Proverbs 29:25 (NIV)

For I hold you by your right hand-I, the LORD your God. And I say to you, 'Don't be afraid. I am here to help you.' Isaiah 41:13

So you have not received a Spirit that makes you fearful slaves. Instead you received God's Spirit when he adopted you as his children. Now we call him, 'Abba, Father.' Romans 8:15

These are a few of the many verses that offer us strength and protection against the enemy's attack. Meditate on these truths and allow God to speak to your heart.

We don't have to shrink back and accept defeat because we are too afraid to pursue victory. We have an answer. We have the armor of God to protect us and help us fight, and we have victory through Jesus Christ and His Word! It is our responsibility though to know His Word, to believe it, and to live according to it. God has given the Bible to us, but we have to read it and study it. Otherwise, it remains inactive in our lives. For example, if we don't know or believe that *'God has given us a spirit of power, and love, and self-discipline'* (2 Timothy 1:7) then we *will* walk around in fear, bound by insecurity.

From the Inside Out

Whenever we feel intimidated, we can be sure that the Spirit of God within us is NOT! He is *never* afraid, *never* intimidated, and *never* insecure. In fact, He is the opposite of those things. *But the Holy Spirit produces this kind of fruit in our lives: love, joy, peace, patience, kindness, goodness, faithfulness, gentleness, and self-control.* Galatians 5:22-23. He is our resource. Every answer is found in Him, and He lives within us. Isn't that amazing? Our privilege is to ask the Holy Spirit to reveal His way to us and then walk in it.

Romans 8:11 says, *The Spirit of God, who raised Jesus from the dead, lives in you. And just as God raised Christ Jesus from the dead, he will give life to your mortal bodies by this same Spirit living within you.*

I absolutely love this verse. You cannot truly grasp it and still walk around feeling insecure! The same Spirit that breathed life into Jesus's physical body breathes life into us! Do we get that? Do we live each day knowing, believing, and *aware* of that fact? I would venture to say probably not on most days. But let's think about what our day would look like if we lived walking in that truth. How would you react to your children, spouse, coworkers, friends, employers, neighbors, family? How differently would you handle your circumstances or view your problems?

It's amazing what God can show us when we quiet our mouths, hearts, and minds long enough to actually hear Him! We are the ones who discount ourselves so quickly. We think we are too old, or too young, not smart enough, not bold enough, not creative enough, not wealthy enough, and the list goes on and on. We could give reason after reason for why God wouldn't choose to work through us. Why not consider what we could do if we actually gave God access to our lives.

Throughout the Bible, God chose people who didn't *feel* qualified.

Abraham felt like he was too old. (Gen. 17:17)

Moses felt like he wasn't a good speaker. (Ex. 4:10)

Jeremiah felt like he was too young. (Jer. 1:6)

Paul felt unworthy. (1 Cor. 15:9)

Jonah felt afraid...that's why he ran. (Book of Jonah) I wouldn't suggest that, given the outcome!

God worked through each of these people, however, to do incredible things for His Kingdom. **The truth is, we allow our insecurity to speak louder than God's Word, and that's a problem!** We praise God with our lips, and we "amen" the great stories we read throughout scripture and hear from various pastors and speakers, yet when it comes to our own lives, we rarely give ourselves a chance to rise up, trust God, and walk in the power He has for us! If we let the indwelling Spirit work through us, keeping our eyes on Him and not on our emotions, we will begin to walk with a lighter step.

She's Living Freedom

Stacey is an amazing woman of God. I have known her for about ten years, and in that time she has been a mentor, sister, and friend to me. She writes,

"My husband and I were in full time ministry for the first 10 years of our marriage. We were the discipleship directors of a large ministry before Joey became the executive pastor of a church. While fulfilling that role, he took on the presidency of an international ministry as well. Everything seemed to be in place. My husband wanted to one day be a lead pastor, but that was not yet on the radar. Then the Lord clearly spoke to us about walking away from it all. We became members of a church where no one knew us. At a meeting to join a small group we were asked to become the leaders.

One night, my husband was unable to be at our meeting, and some of the ladies started questioning me about decisions we had made. Those close to me know that I can easily be pressured into changing my mind/actions/thoughts if anyone is not happy with me. Somehow I have tricked myself into believing that it is possible to make everyone happy. I have "sold out" my husband and myself trying to make this happen. Sad I know! Because we had walked away from everything, I hadn't felt this kind of pressure in a while. I kindly told them to take these concerns up with Joey and walked to my car as fast as possible.

In the car I broke down. This seems so juvenile, but it was as if my insecurity was choking me. I was immediately attacked with thoughts from the enemy. How could I be a pastor's wife with all these insecurities? No wonder God had us walk away from everything. I was so messed up. Maybe Joey married the wrong person.

Going back to when we had resigned, one of the hardest things about walking away from the church was the disappointment it would caused so many people to have in me. In those first few days the Lord gave me this scripture. Proverbs 29:25 says *The fear of human opinion disables; trusting in God protects you from that.* While driving home the night of the confrontation with the ladies, His Spirit quickened my mind to understand this. I was being disabled by human opinion. Why did it matter so much to me? I put my daughters in bed that night and got out my Bible and a prayer book by Beth Moore. It was as if the Lord was waiting for me to be ready to deal with this insecurity. I had dealt with the symptoms but not the root. I learned that night that my biggest need is unconditional love. NO ONE can fulfill that need except God, and I shouldn't expect them to. I had the mindset, however, that my value was only based on what I could do for others. If I was doing or sacrificing for them, then I felt like I gained their love and commitment. No one else can give us unfailing love. It's impossible.

So every day, and I mean *every* day, I set aside time to allow God to fill me with His love and His Word. If I don't, I find myself in a battle for the love of others, and that will never fulfill. I can, like the scripture says, trust Him. When I choose to trust Him, I am protected from disabling insecurity."

Remember, God doesn't always remove our insecurity. He shows us how to *fight* it and how to see Him and ourselves differently. As we spend time learning and applying God's Word, we will gain freedom from our insecurity and fear every time they pop up!

Let's pray:

Lord, there are times in my life where I still feel like that little girl hiding behind my father's legs because I'm too shy and scared to come out. But I know that You have called me out. You have created me to be a victorious woman, and although I know You're still working on me, help me to remember that You are always with me. You have created me for a purpose that You have chosen me to live out. You have chosen me! That's an amazing concept, and I am humbled and in awe. Thank You for loving me and for giving me the tools I need to keep fighting and to live in freedom. I will not give up!

Chapter 2 Reflection

In what ways has insecurity kept you bound?

_____

_____

_____

_____

Have there been times when you've either withdrawn from or attacked people in your life? Can you look back and see where insecurity had a part to play in those encounters?

_____

_____

_____

_____

Have you ever held back from doing something you know God wanted you do because you felt too afraid? Can you see where those choices can begin to turn into disobedience?

_____

_____

_____

_____

Read the Scriptures mentioned throughout this chapter again to remind yourself that God has not created you to live in insecurity. What are some things you are realizing from reading these verses?

_____

_____

_____

_____

_____

CHAPTER 3

Old Wounds

*M*y parents were never married, and they separated soon after I was born. I lived mainly with my mom, visiting my dad for summers, holidays, and special occasions. My mom accepted Christ as her Savior when I was young, so I grew up being very involved in church, asking Jesus into my own heart at the age of five. My dad only lived a few hours away, and I talked to him regularly. He also had two other daughters from previous marriages, and both were several years older than me. Every summer, Christmas, and Easter, my older sister and I would go to our dad's house. These were very enjoyable times. We went on vacations, hung out at the house, and spent time together. During spring break of my fourth grade year, my dad whisked me away to Disney World. It was just the two of us. Little did I know that trip would be our last time together.

For years, my father had been suffering from Bipolar Disorder or Manic Depression, caused by a chemical imbalance in his brain. At the time, I was too young to know that. A month after that Disney World trip, a policeman showed up at my mom's townhouse one night. She sent me into another room while the two of them talked, but I soon found out that my dad's body had been found in his garage. He had committed suicide.

When I heard the news, I remember falling to my knees sobbing and shaking. My life was forever changed, and the road from there was a very painful one. I clearly remember the pain of the reality of death settling in as we followed the casket out of the church after the funeral. I wanted to scream for them to stop wheeling my daddy away because then he really would be gone, but all I could do was put one foot in front of the other and walk outside. Part of me wanted to crawl on top of the casket and be buried with him. During the next year, I recall waking up and for the first few moments forgetting that he had died. Then I'd remember and feel a sense of dread sweep over me again.

As a ten-year-old, I wasn't sure how to deal with every-thing. All I knew was that I hated people feeling sorry for me. So instead of talking about my pain and raw feelings, I buried them. I quickly learned how to pretend that nothing was wrong. The only person I felt that I could really talk to was my older sister because she understood, but those conversations were few and far between. She was nine years older than me, so when he died, she was nineteen. I felt jealous that she had spent more time with him than I had. It wasn't fair. As the years went by, I got better and better at burying my emotions. Although I thought this was my solution, the truth is that the more I tried *not* to let my dad's death affect me, the more it did. I reached a point where I could smile around people but whenever I was alone, I would fall apart.

Because I was becoming depressed myself, during my junior year in high school I began to drink to keep my heart numb, and I put up walls to keep it guarded. By my senior year, I was drinking a lot, and feeling more and more out of control. Drinking became my way of escape. I didn't want to open up to or need anyone, including God. I wanted to be self-sufficient and independent so nobody could hurt, disappoint, or leave me again. I never blamed myself for his death, but I think what I felt after he died was worse.

I lived my life for many years convinced that I was *not good enough*. I knew my dad had to have thought about me before he ended his life, but the fact that he hadn't changed his mind and took his life anyway was a torment! I felt ashamed as well because I thought other people must have been wondering what was wrong with me.

I got to the point where I didn't even like myself, and I was afraid for other people to see who I really was. I feared no one else would like me either. The enemy whispered those lies into my soul, and I believed them for a long time. I also felt a lot of anger. I was angry at my dad because he chose this path. He chose to end his life, and let me grow up without him. I was angry at God because I felt like He could have stopped this from happening, but He didn't. And I was angry at myself for not being lovable enough to make my dad want to live. After years of living like this, I was worn out and exhausted.

I was never meant to carry my burden alone, but my pain led me to walk that lonely road. One night I found myself at my lowest point, knowing I could no longer go on living the way I had been. My mom was at a woman's retreat that weekend, and I was supposed to be at a cheerleading sleepover at my best friend's house. Once there, however, I couldn't fake a smile. Instead I drove myself home in the pouring rain, crying the whole time. I got to my house, sank to the living room floor, and wept. I didn't want to feel that way, but I didn't know what to do about it. My best friend kept calling me until I finally answered, and her parents ended up coming over to talk with me. They shared their concern about the pain I was holding onto and the decisions I was making. They offered wisdom, love, and support. That night, I realized how much I needed God's strength and love, and I desperately needed His healing. Yet I still wasn't sure how to go about everything.

We never seem to see it at the time, but God has our steps ordered, and He is just waiting for us to ask for His help!

I wasn't quite at the point of asking for His help yet, but I soon would be. Somehow the administration at the Christian high school I was attending found out about my drinking habit. I ended up with a lot of consequences, some of which included a percentage of my grades being taken away and not being able to walk down the aisle at my graduation. Among other things, I was also suspended. I got angry at first, but this actually became a turning point for me. It wasn't a complete 180-degree turn around, but I began to understand that I really *had* to change. I needed to make better choices about my relationships and habits.

I decided to go away for college that fall. I went to Gardner-Webb University in North Carolina. There I began attending therapy sessions with an incredible Christian counselor. I didn't want to go at first, but none of my own efforts had helped, so I decided to give it a try. One day she asked me, "Alison, what do you want the end result of these sessions to be?" The only answer I could give her was that I wanted to feel "okay." I wanted to feel "normal." Although I couldn't completely describe how normal would feel, I knew it couldn't involve feeling constant pain. I told her I felt like I was dangling from a cliff and although I wanted to be on the other side; I didn't know how to get there. I felt like if I *could* get there, I'd be all right. She helped me see so much in the span of a few months, and I finally began to work through and talk about my pain. I wasn't actively living for God at the time, but my counselor had given me some homework to do before my next session. I actually decided that day to pray about the things she had asked me to think about. I sat on a wooden bench swing outside my dorm, and that day, I clearly and lovingly heard the Lord whisper to my heart, "It wasn't about you."

Such a short but profound statement. In that moment, my chains were broken, and for the first time in nine years I began to see the situation differently. I realized my father's death had nothing to do with me not being good enough. It was about *his* struggle, and he lost his battle. That truth didn't make his death feel less sad, but it did free me from the incredible bondage that I had been carrying around. The fact that God would speak freedom to my heart in a season of life where I was making wrong choices was also healing. I realized how much God truly loved me. He was more concerned with the state of my heart than my actions. Like a hurt child, I was rebelling to try to get back at God, the One I felt had hurt me. But He had never abandoned me, and He was not intimidated by all my feelings.

God is big enough to handle our pain! Many times people don't know how to respond to stories of brokenness. They don't know what to do with shattered lives, but God does! In His loving mercy, He reached out to my damaged heart and spoke healing and freedom. He longed to heal those hurting places in me. I surrendered everything to God, *including* my pain, questions, anger, and fears, and decided to trust Him. As I did, He brought the healing I so desperately needed. This didn't happen overnight, but it did happen.

Now, I am a completely different woman. I have experienced God's healing and grace. I have found the love of a father in my Heavenly Father, which has radically transformed my life! Letting go of my wounds was not easy, especially since I'd been carrying them for years, but the outcome *far o*utweighs the pain of the process.

The Pain

The ability to feel pain is a sign that we are still alive. Sometimes an event can be so disastrous, so traumatic that we wonder if we'll ever survive it, but if we are feeling the pain, we are indeed a survivor. God has more for us though than just survival! If the sensation of pain is there, so is the hope for the healing.

What we do with our wounds determines our quality of life thereafter. Consider this. If you had an open gash on your arm, would you cover it up and medicate it several times a day for the rest of your life, or would you go and allow the doctor to stitch it up to ensure proper healing? The first option would be dangerous because if treated improperly, infection could set, the wound would not close well, and a full recovery most likely would never happen. Most of us would allow the doctor to do his work. Why? Because even though that would cause some pain as well, it wouldn't be nearly as painful as leaving a gaping wound.

In our spiritual and emotional lives we need to realize this principle as well. Many times we cover our broken places so people will not see them, but in doing that, we don't deal with them. We don't acknowledge them or take the steps we need to for healing to occur. **Many of us are walking around settling for sympathy when we could be receiving healing!**

Most of us have endured suffering to one degree or another, including regret, loss, abuse, rejection, a broken heart, a fractured family, or all of the above. We have felt the shock that comes with it. So often we allow our brokenness to determine our identity. We make decisions about the present and future based on our past, hiding behind the same walls of defense we built so long ago. We remain in bondage, weighed down because we haven't allowed God to mend our wounds.

If we want to walk in freedom, we have to *surrender* everything to God and allow Him to heal us. If we do not deal with our pain and allow God to work through it with us, we will never experience His healing. We will never see our lives fully turned around.

Many times when I have shared my story with someone who knows me now, I hear a response like, "I never would have guessed that about you." That makes me very aware of two facts. First, the people with whom we come into contact also have stories we could never guess. Some who smile do so to hide their inner pain. Many whom we think have their lives well put together have gone through very difficult circumstances. We can't judge by the outward appearance, which is something God warns us about in His Word. Second, **when God changes a life, He changes it!** He doesn't halfway heal. He doesn't partially put people back together. He *completely* restores, and gives back even more than what we lost! Thank God!

Typical Reaction

We can easily become angry at God when painful events happen. We feel like He could have and should have prevented them. We want to blame someone. Trust often gets shattered in painful times, and we tend to pull away from God. We can become deceived into thinking that if we don't trust anyone, including God, we can be in control. We won't get hurt. We won't get disappointed. However, withdrawal **never** actually brings freedom! We weren't meant to carry the burdens of life on our own, and when we choose to, we get weighed down. 1 Peter 5:7 says, *"Give all your worries and cares to God, for he cares about you."* God wants to carry that extra weight for us. He knows what to do with it! He knows how to handle our suffering, and how to get us through life, but we have to let Him.

The Truth of the Situation

We never can truly control all the events in our lives. We live in a fallen world! Bad things can and do happen to all of us. None of us are promised a life without pain. God never guaranteed that when we follow Him, we would become exempt from attack. Yet so many Christians feel this way. Actually the Word of God prepares and equips us for hard times.

John 16:33 says, *I have told you all this so that you may have peace in me. Here on earth you will have many trials and sorrow. But take heart, because I have overcome the world.*

Jesus is saying that as long as we live on Earth, life will not always be easy. We will face hard, painful, and difficult times.

Psalm 23:4 says, *Even when I walk through the darkest valley, I will not be afraid, for you are close beside me. Your rod and your staff protect and comfort me.*

There are times when we find ourselves in this valley, physically, emotionally, or spiritually. God doesn't promise us a way around every hard situation, but we do have the assurance that He is with us *in* those moments! Also we could look at Ephesians again.

Ephesians 6:13 says, *Therefore, put on every piece of God's armor so you will be able to resist the enemy in the time of evil. Then after the battle you will still be standing firm.*

This verse says "*in* the time of evil" not "just in case evil comes near you." We are in a spiritual battle, and a battle guarantees some hard times! War is never easy. We are promised an outcome of victory, but that doesn't mean we won't get some scars along the way.

God is good all the time, but He doesn't go around with a magic wand waving away all the bad in our lives. Instead, He *walks* us through it. He *heals* us in the midst of it. He *redeems* the broken places. He *restores* our souls. He turns our hurts around and brings forth His will in our lives. Romans 8:28 (Amplified Bible) says, *We are assured and know that [God being a partner in their labor] all things work together and are [fitting into a plan] for good to and for those who love God and are called according to [His] design and purpose.* **He has a plan to create beauty from the mess!**

We can't control what happens to us in this life, but we can control our reactions, and how we allow them to shape our future. So whether our pain has come from situations and events beyond our control, or from our own poor choices, God is a God of healing and restoration!

I have gotten to a point where I realize that no matter if we serve God or not, hard times come. Without God, we only have ourselves to get us through. Many of us have tried that route and experienced the exhaustion and depression brought about by our own feeble efforts. With God, however, we have strength, power, hope, joy, and the promise of victory in the end! The journey to healing is not an easy one, nor is it usually a quick one. However, this journey is definitely worth taking. **You *can* walk in freedom from your pain!**

She's Living Freedom

Sharon, my Pastor's wife, has an incredible life story. She has been through a lot, but God has redeemed her wounds and is allowing her to minister to so many. She writes,

"As an infant, my mother was physically and mentally unable to take care of my three year old brother and me. My brother was raised by my maternal grandparents after my parents divorced. My father took me as an infant to his parents in Oklahoma where I was raised until I was about 10 years old. At age four, I was diagnosed with bulbar polio with paralysis setting in. A spinal tap was done and I was placed in an iron lung. I was terrified by what was happening. Hospitalization and being left alone in a dark room left me crying through the nights. At around this same age, I was molested by a neighbor. This was a traumatic experience that I would deal with later in my life. The doctors told my grandparents that I would be crippled and in a wheelchair for the rest of my life. Although, I had one leg noticeably shorter than the other, the Lord touched me through the prayers of the little church where we attended, and through my grandfather's old fashioned way of physical therapy. At that young impressive age, I would tell people that I had three moms; a birth mom, a step-mom, and a grandmom. Guess I was just looking for a mother's love.

At 10 years of age, I moved from Oklahoma to Baltimore. The transition from the country to the city left me very sad and confused. I now lived with a step-mother I did not know, a father who had visited yearly, and a new school with city kids. The unfamiliarity of everything in this new life made me feel alone. As a child, I was ashamed that I did not have a mother like other children. I felt abandoned by both of my parents. Guilt clouded my ability to feel loved by anyone much less a heavenly Father. I wish I would have known the words found in PS 27:10 (Amp) that says *'though my father and mother have forsaken me, yet the Lord will adopt me as His child.'*

As the years went by, our family moved from Baltimore to Florida and eventually Arizona. There, at the age of 19, I met my future husband. During our courtship, we discussed both the good and bad experiences that had happened in my life. I was afraid that upon revealing my past, this young man who had come from a very solid family, might not want to be with someone like me who was ashamed of her past experiences. He assured me of his love for me, and we were married. So much baggage can be carried into a marriage. On the inside, I wondered if my husband would change his mind about loving me or if he would leave me like my dad had done, but he only showed his unwavering love for me.

After having our second child at age 25, I received Christ as my Savior. I received His forgiveness for my sins, but I still felt unworthy to receive God's love. My new journey began with many new lessons showing me that I was chosen even before I was born; that God knit me together in my mother's womb and that I was wonderfully made by Him. (Psalm 139:13-16) Though we have earthly parents, God is our Maker and His love sustains us and makes us whole as we begin the process of healing the painful and broken parts of our lives. I began to trust the Lord because He said that He would never leave me or forsake me. I saw how He had placed a wonderful husband in my life to love and support me. The Lord had healed me physically when I had polio.

I saw God's protection even when I didn't know He was there. He showed me that I was not at fault for the emotional and physical damages that happened to me as a child. I was once filled with shame and felt unloved and unworthy. However, with forgiveness for others and myself, I was set free. No more shame, no more rejection, no more unforgiveness; only His love.

I do not blame anyone for my life's circumstances; this is simply 'my story.' We are not to dwell on the past but to learn from it. As a little girl, I believed I would marry a preacher. It's amazing that God fulfilled that dream in my life by calling my husband to close our business and start a new church in Scottsdale, Arizona where we currently pastor. We must let the springs of new life flourish in us so we may be complete in Him."

Let's pray:

Father, thank You that You do turn all things around for the good of those who love You! Thank You for the whole heart that You offer me in return for my shattered one. I know that Your healing touch can reach even the deepest areas of pain in my life. Thank You for the future You have for me in exchange for my broken past. Most of all, Lord, thank You for walking me through each and every day of my life. You've never abandoned me. I love You Father so much. I will no longer settle for sympathy; I will trust You for complete healing. Although I may never know all the answers, I know I can trust Your Spirit to guide me and restore me. Continue to take me down the path You have chosen for me. Help me follow Your lead and be obedient every step along the way.

Chapter 3 Reflection

Are there any wounds in your past that you haven't dealt with? If so, what are they?_____

_____

_____

_____

_____

What caused these wounds? And how do they affect you now?

_____

_____

_____

_____

_____

Have you pulled away from God feeling as if He has disappointed you?_____

_____

_____

_____

_____

Are you aware that there are many verses in the Bible that prepare you to walk through hard times? If not, I encourage you to find them. Start by re-reading the ones listed in this chapter. What things stand out to you in these verses?

_____

_____

_____

_____

Take some time to pray and ask for God's Healing to begin to work in your heart and life.

CHAPTER 4

Complacency

I started this book shortly after my first son was born. I had been in full-time ministry with my husband, and when I had our baby, my schedule changed quite a bit. I wasn't able to be on the go with him all the time anymore. I had to slow down and refocus my priorities. For a while, I was overwhelmed. Then I started watching television…a lot! I had never been home so much before. I'd watch it while I was nursing or while he was napping. I found myself watching close to four hours of television a day, all the while feeling like I never had any time!

I clearly remember one morning being frustrated and stuck in a rut, unsure how to get out. I was in the shower praying and feeling sorry for myself that I didn't have as much time for ministry anymore. I was questioning all the dreams and goals I had for my life that I believed God had put in my heart. Writing was one of them, and I felt the Holy Spirit ask me what I was waiting for. I stood there in the shower thinking, "Well I just had a baby, I don't have any time to write!" That's when it hit me how much time I had been spending watching pointless TV shows. Lack of time wasn't my real problem. I kept thinking "one day" I will write a book, as though there would be a "perfect" day to start; however, as God began to speak to my heart, **I realized "one day" begins when I choose to discipline myself *today*!**

I needed to turn off the television and start doing what God had put in my heart to do. So I did, and for a while, writing was going well. Then when my son was six months old, I found out, to my surprise, that I was pregnant again! My writing took a backseat to morning sickness, and I didn't start back up for quite some time. The ministry we had worked with for seven years relocated out of state, and after seeking the Lord for direction, we decided not to move with them. My husband got hired at a different church in our area, and a few months later, our second son was born. Life became even more of a whirlwind! We were directing a smaller, full-time, discipleship program for young adults, as well as the youth and college pastors at our church. Our schedule was non-stop for about two years, and we were exhausted. Again, I felt stuck in a rut. We were not accomplishing the dreams God had put in our hearts to do. We felt as if we were spinning our wheels but going nowhere.

Thankfully God led us through some major changes in those ministry positions, and in the middle of it all, I found out I was pregnant *again!* I had a son who was about to turn three, one who wasn't quite two, and I was having our third son. We knew God's hand was in the transition taking place in our lives, but we weren't quite sure what the future held.

I typically do not enjoy major changes, especially when I'm pregnant and more emotional, but as I fervently began seeking the Lord, I felt the Holy Spirit again challenging me to discipline myself in my writing. Now, I am definitely not a super mom! I knew I did not have a lot of time, but I did have *some* time, and I *could* use it to write. My goal became to write for thirty minutes three times a week. Most weeks I was able to, some I wasn't, but I was becoming more disciplined and learning to push through!

Former president Jimmy Carter once said, "I hate to see complacency prevail in our lives when it's so directly contrary to the teaching of Christ."[2]

Complacency *is* contrary to the life that God has chosen for us. It is contrary to a life of freedom. Most of us have days where we could best describe our feelings as "blah." However, when these days run together and become the norm, we have a problem. Complacency is starting to creep in. When that happens, we stop moving forward. We may go through the motions of life, but at best we're living in mediocrity, which is never what God intended. As women of God, we need to *snap out* of that lifestyle because we were created for more! Many times, we give up on the hope that there is more, but there is.

Remember John 10:10? *The thief does not come except to steal, and to kill, and to destroy. I have come that they may have life, and that they may have it more abundantly.* We can't have an abundant life if we aren't truly living! If we are just drifting through our days, or stuck in a rut, the enemy is stealing life from us.

Push Through

The way out of complacency is through discipline and determination. We literally have to push through it, just like losing weight in the physical realm. A lot of our weight gain comes from becoming too comfortable! We don't bother exercising or eating healthy. Discipline either wears off or was never there, and as a result, our waistlines expand! To lose the weight, we have to choose to change our eating habits and push ourselves to work out. While working out, we have to go beyond what is comfortable. That is the only way to get results.

Spiritually, it's exactly the same. If we want to live a life of freedom, we will have to move beyond our comfort zones. We must discipline ourselves in how we manage our time to include prayer and Bible study. We need to pay attention to our thoughts and attitudes and how those affect our actions. We need to establish goals and find ways to work on them regularly. Let's not go through life on "autopilot." Let's be determined to *stay* disciplined! As we do these things, we will continue to grow in our relationship with our Heavenly Father, causing us to grow in freedom.

We can be women who push beyond our feelings, who don't give up, who don't allow complacency in our spiritual lives, our marriages, our friendships, our relationships with our children, our work, or our goals. We often have a million excuses for why we can't push through, but let's ask ourselves what we *can* do. Let's discipline ourselves to start somewhere!

1 Corinthians 9:24-27 (The Message) says, *You've all been to the stadium and seen the athletes race. Everyone runs; one wins. Run to win. All good athletes train hard. They do it for a gold medal that tarnishes and fades. You're after one that's gold eternally. I don't know about you, but I'm running hard for the finish line. I'm giving it everything I've got. No sloppy living for me! I'm staying alert and in top condition. I'm not going to get caught napping, telling everyone else all about it and then missing out myself.*

What a powerful Scripture! It's definitely not one we always *want* to hear but one that will help us beat this lackadaisical way of life. Let's live by that Scripture. "No sloppy living" for God's girls! Get out of that comfort zone. Push through!

She's Living Freedom

My good friend Elisia has faced the challenge of complacency as well and writes,

"I currently work as a co-manager for a well-known retail company, and I must admit that complacency is something that can easily slip into my life. I work most weekends, and to be honest the one Sunday I may have off a month, I don't always feel like going to church. The dictionary defines complacency as: '1. A feeling of contentment or self-satisfaction, especially when coupled with an unawareness of danger, trouble, or controversy.'

The word that sticks out to me is "unawareness." We can get so caught up in the demands of work, family, and whatever life may bring. We may have good intentions to read the Bible, pray, or go to church; but, when it comes to that moment, we are often too tired or don't feel like it, and so we don't go. Before we know it, that missed moment has turned into days, weeks, and maybe even months without Bible study, prayer, or church. These things are vital to our spiritual growth and affect our everyday life decisions. We may feel like we are doing okay in the moment, but we have to realize that "unawareness of danger, trouble, or controversy" may be closer than we think.

I am battling complacency by choosing to be fiercely committed to my relationship with God. It starts with a decision. The Bible says in Joshua 24:15 (NIV) *'Choose for yourselves this day whom you will serve.'* Like any friendship or relationship you must consistently choose to be committed. For me, my relationship with God means everything, and I don't want anything to shake it! I realize that God will never fail me, and I will only fail if I quit! I choose not to let complacency rule my life!"

Let's Pray:

Father I want to be the woman You have created me to be! I want to run the race You have set before me, and I'm tired of the frustration that comes from not living in my purpose. Thank You for giving me the strength and the grace to be disciplined. Help me to push through my feelings, my routine, and my comfort zone! I know you have great plans for me! Please give me the strength to use what I have and the time and resources I have, to start somewhere. I know You are always faithful! Today I determine to live a life of discipline! I love you!

Chapter 4 Reflection

In what areas of your life has complacency, or as 1 Corinthians 9 puts it, "sloppy living," started to creep in?_____

_____

_____

_____

_____

Are there goals/dreams/visions that you have for your life that are just sitting idle? List them._____

_____

_____

_____

_____

What are some things that you can start doing NOW to push forward in different areas of your life?_____

_____

_____

_____

_____

_____

CHAPTER 5

Misconceptions

ou know that nervous feeling you get in the pit of your stomach when a police officer is driving behind you? As a young adult I realized that even though I grew up in church that was exactly how I had come to view God. Partly, I was thankful He was there in case I needed help, but mostly I felt like He was a cop, following me waiting for me to mess up. Where did that misunderstanding come from? It came from a *lack of knowledge*. I didn't really know who God was, and I wasn't actively trying to find out! I was seeing Him through my fear, pain, and insecurities.

The way we perceive God will determine the way that we serve Him. If we don't understand the heart of God, we will never be free. Instead, we will always look at Him with a clouded perspective. The *World English Dictionary* defines misconception as "a false or mistaken view, opinion, or attitude." These misconceptions occur when we choose to see God through our natural eyes and in light of *our* personal perspectives, feelings, circumstances, and other relationships. We have to look internally and figure out how we view God. Do we see Him as angry, passive, unfair, uninvolved, someone to appease or perform for? Misunderstanding God is so damaging because it affects the way we live and hinders our daily relationship with the Father.

Misconceptions About God

A lot of times we feel like we have to do something to get God's attention. We see children do this all the time with their parents. They either act out and rebel, or they try to do and say everything perfectly.

Many of us do this in our relationship with God. To merit God's consideration, we feel like we have to perform properly, pray a certain amount of time, cry, beg, plead, or get mad. But the thing is, God's attention is *already* on us.

Doing all those things only twists our perception of Him more and hinders us from really being able to connect with our Father who is waiting for us to come to Him and spend time with Him. He doesn't need all the added "flare." He just wants us. Instead of trying to *get* God's attention, we need to remember that, as His children, we *already* have it.

Another common misconception is that when things are going great in our lives, we can "feel" as though maybe it has to do with how much we are pleasing God. On the other hand, when things are difficult, or we go through something we don't understand like an illness, a job loss, the death of a loved one, or a financial crisis we can sometimes mistakenly view our trials as God's favor being withdrawn from us.

We begin to wonder what we've done wrong, how we've upset God, or where we missed the mark in our walk with Him. These thought patterns carry so much deception, and put too much focus on what we've done or haven't done, than on our relationship with God and what He's done. Our relationship with Him is a *daily* walk of grace, which means sometimes we make right choices, and sometimes we don't and find ourselves needing more of His grace, strength, and forgiveness. In times when we need those things, God doesn't love us any less! He is not sitting on His throne frowning down on us, with His arms crossed, irritated that we failed. Yet how many times do we live as if that's the kind of God we serve?

God is a God of grace. Most believers and unbelievers alike have heard that, but as Christians, do we understand what grace truly is? Grace is unmerited favor. Grace is getting what we don't deserve! Grace is God being good to us, when we deserve punishment. It's God offering us life when we deserve death. It's God's love when we deserve His wrath. Grace is favor that we did not merit, that we did nothing to earn! So why do we go around thinking and living (even if won't admit to it) that when we fail, God must not love us or want to bless us? If He only loved us when we pleased Him, that wouldn't be grace! If He only blessed us when we pleased Him, that wouldn't be grace either. No matter what we do or don't do, as children of God we are loved and cared for. Many of us know the Scriptures on grace, yet we still live as though it is something we have to earn and keep on earning.

A Great Example

The Israelites are a great example of God's patience, love, and mercy. They continually turned their backs on Him from the moment He set out to deliver them. He rescued them, provided for them, loved them, spoke to them and cared for them, and yet every time they couldn't understand or immediately see His plan, they freaked out! They questioned His deliverance and His care. **They longed to go back to the familiar even though it meant bondage, instead of trusting God for the unknown with the promise of freedom attached to it!**

We can read the stories and think, "What was wrong with them? How could they be so stubborn and forgetful?" But if we are honest, we can also see ourselves in them. How many times has God faithfully brought us through difficult circumstances, and then the very next hard situation we are in, we question His faithfulness again? We ask, "Lord, don't You see what I'm going through? Where are You?" We worry and complain because we don't have the answer; we can't see what God is working out on our behalf. We aren't sure how we are going to get through what we are facing, just like the Israelites.

One day I was reading and came across a passage that gave me an "aha!" moment. Psalm 106: 40-48 (NKJV) says, *Therefore the wrath of the LORD was kindled against His people, so that He abhorred His own inheritance. And He gave them into the hand of the Gentiles, and those who hated them ruled over them. Their enemies also oppressed them, and they were brought into subjection under their hand. Many times He delivered them; but they rebelled in their counsel, and were brought low for their iniquity. Nevertheless He regarded their affliction, When He heard their cries and for their sake He remembered His covenant, And relented according to the multitude of His mercies. He also made them to be pitied by all those who carried them away captive. Save us, O LORD our God, and gather us from among the Gentiles, to give thanks to Your holy name, to triumph in Your praise. Blessed be the LORD God of Israel from everlasting to everlasting! And let all the people say, 'Amen!'"*

No matter how rebellious, stubborn, and foolish the Israelites were God always came through for them every time they repented and came back to Him! *Every time!* Honestly, their story began to annoy me a little. I would get so frustrated at how foolish they were, but then I realized how thankful I am that I serve the same God! He is exactly like that with all of us. Sin carries consequences, yet through Jesus we now have forgiveness, grace, and access to God in a way the people in the Old Testament never had. However, even then, God's love and grace were shown in that He always rescued His own when they called on Him!

Now, more than being frustrated at the Israelites, I'm relieved that God's grace can reach even the most stubborn sinners. Their story should give us all hope! Look again at Psalm 106:44-46 which begins with "nevertheless." What an amazing word! We mess up and get off track, but "nevertheless" when God hears our **repentant** cry He answers! I also love how this phrase says "according to the *multitude* of His mercies." Let that sink in for a moment. We can't run out of His mercy! He is constantly saving us from the mistakes, circumstances, and stubbornness that weigh us down!

James 4:8 (NKJV) says, *Draw near to God and He will draw near to you.* We can see this principle at work. When the Israelites drew near to God, He came through for them every time. When they turned their backs on Him and walked away, they wound up in trouble. This is true for us today as well. When we draw near to God, He reveals Himself to us. He never leaves us, the Bible makes that clear, but *we* have to draw near to *Him*. We have to take that step. When we do, we will see God in ways we haven't before.

Grace is by no means an excuse to sin or live consistently in a way that we know displeases God. Romans 6:1-3 says, *What shall we say then? Shall we continue in sin that grace may abound? Certainly not! How shall we who died to sin live any longer in it? Or do you not know that as many of us as were baptized into Christ Jesus were baptized into His death?*

Grace is not the cover-up for a rebellious lifestyle. I'm not talking right now to the people who are trying to find a way into Heaven without submitting their lives, wills, and daily actions to the obedience of Jesus Christ. I'm talking to the people who have done and are doing that, who desire to live a life that pleases God, but are somehow missing the reality of God's love and grace for them. **I'm talking to the Christians who are weighed down and struggling to understand how passionately loved and pursued they are by Almighty God on their *best days* as well as on their *worst days*!**

Misconceptions About People

The way we respond towards people can also weigh us down sometimes and steal our freedom. **People are not the enemy! The enemy is the enemy, and people are people!** We very often confuse these things, and when we do, we fall right into the devil's trap. Paul reminds us in Ephesians 6:12, *"For we are not fighting against flesh-and-blood enemies, but against evil rulers and authorities of the unseen world,*

*against mighty powers in this dark world, and against evil
spirits in the heavenly places."*

People seem like an easier target for us to fight against.
Especially as women, we can develop quite an attitude when
we want to put a face to the offenses we have suffered, but
the Bible shows us, that it's not "flesh and blood" we should
be fighting against. We fight against the enemy, the devil.

Yes, people quite often fail and disappoint us. Also,
because everyone has a free will and may choose to follow
their own sinful desires, they can end up causing great dev-
astation for themselves and others.

I'm not trying to minimize what you may have suffered
or experienced; I only want us to view these things through
our spiritual eyes. As children of God, that's what we have to
do! We can't just apply the promises and principles that we
like or that benefit us. If we believe the Bible, then we believe
the whole Bible, even the parts that are very hard to live out!
Forgiving others by not allowing ourselves to become bitter
when offended is the best example. Our human nature is bent
on blame, bitterness, criticism, jealousy, revenge, offense,
and holding grudges. Thankfully, God has given us the
Holy Spirit and through His power we are enabled to realize
the truth! Fighting people will not bring positive results or

freedom! We must become women who understand how to deal with this misconception. We handle it through prayer. We ask God for strength. **We extend grace, and we fight the enemy, not each other!**

Misconceptions About Ourselves

Many times we place added weight on ourselves through unrealistic expectations, guilt, comparison, and busyness. We get an idea in our minds of what we are "supposed" to be doing, "supposed" to look like, what people want from us, and what God expects from us. Well, these ideas are often wrong! The more we try to conform to our own and others' expectations, the more unnecessary weight we end up carrying around.

Comparing ourselves with others is a big issue with women of all ages and is so detrimental to our freedom. God works in each of our lives at different times and in different ways. If we're busy looking at the people around us to see what they're doing, we miss what He is showing us about ourselves.

Like I stated earlier, my husband and I worked with a discipleship ministry for many years. We had long days and worked with a lot of students. When I got pregnant with our first son, I experienced severe morning sickness lasting all day, so I spent most of the first 5 months of my pregnancy in our apartment throwing up. My "normal" life slowed to a different pace. I had to start doing things differently, and during that waiting time, I had to make room in my life for what God was doing in me. I was in the same place physically as all the other leadership we worked with, headed in the same general direction, but individually God was doing something different in my personal life. Now there were days that I compared myself to others around me, feeling like they were getting more opportunities and becoming better leaders. I was often weighed down by jealousy and insecurity. My excitement over this amazing miracle of our first child was wearing off because I got caught in the trap of comparison. This confession sounds extremely foolish now, but that's exactly what happened when I compared myself to others. I got caught in a trap that distorted my vision and perspective, and stole my freedom and joy.

We can't compare our walk with God or our calling with anyone else's. He is faithful, and He works in and through each of us according to His timing! We have to remember our Father knows exactly what we need, and He knows how to get us there.

Misconceptions About Freedom

There are many mistaken beliefs about freedom, but there are two I want to highlight in this book. First is the misconception that freedom means doing whatever we want whenever we want. Let's look at what the Word of God says about freedom in a few passages.

1 Corinthians 10:22-24: *What? Do we dare to rouse the Lord's jealousy? Do you think we are stronger than he is? You say, 'I am allowed to do anything'—but not everything is good for you. You say, 'I am allowed to do anything'—but not everything is beneficial. Don't be concerned for your own good but for the good of others."*

Galatians 3:21-22 says, *Is there a conflict, then, between God's law and God's promises? Absolutely not! If the law could give us new life, we could be made right with God by obeying it. But the Scriptures declare that we are all prisoners of sin, so we receive God's promise of freedom only by believing in Jesus Christ.*

The Bible says the only way we truly obtain freedom is by believing in Jesus. We are bound by sin until we do that. When we come to Him, He gives us *liberty* and *deliverance* from that lifestyle, freeing us to live outside the things that weigh us down! He frees us from sin, but does not give us a pass to do whatever we want!

Galatians 5:13 says, *For you have been called to live in freedom, my brothers and sisters. But don't use your freedom to satisfy your sinful nature. Instead, use your freedom to serve one another in love."*

When we use freedom as a way to serve our own desires, it becomes selfishness, which traps and deceives us into thinking we are free, when truly we become bound to those desires. That is why the last admonition in Galatians 5:13 is so important. True freedom comes only from believing in Jesus and walking in His ways!

The second misconception about freedom is that it can't possibly come from serving God. In fact, many would think the words "Christian" and "freedom" don't belong together. They view Christianity as a burdensome list of rules, but nothing could be farther from the truth! Jesus paid the ultimate sacrifice so that we could be free and walk in that freedom! 1 Timothy 2:6 says, *He gave his life to purchase freedom for everyone. This is the message God gave to the world at just the right time.*

Galatians 5:7-9 says, *You were running the race so well. Who has held you back from following the truth? **It certainly*** *isn't God, for he is the one who called you to freedom. This false teaching is like a little yeast that spreads through the whole batch of dough!* (emphasis mine)

I grew up in Virginia and have visited Washington, DC many times. I love all the history that is represented there. One of my favorite memorials is the Korean War memorial. My grandpa fought in that war, and thankfully made it out alive. He was a paratrooper instructor, teaching soldiers how to jump out of airplanes onto the battlefield below. The morning he was scheduled to ship out to Korea, he was late, arriving minutes after his company of soldiers had left. He was placed with another group, which turned out to be a miracle, because not one of the men he was originally supposed to be with survived!

The granite sign at that memorial reads "Freedom Isn't Free." What a powerful statement. Countless men and women have lost their lives throughout the years to ensure this country's freedom. They paid the price, while the rest of us get to enjoy the benefits. The same is true spiritually. Jesus Christ paid the price for our freedom with His life! He sacrificed Himself so we could have abundant life. Do we live as though that sacrifice was in vain? Do we think the price Christ paid was not enough? He died, so that we might live.

Are we really living? He has called us to freedom. Religion and legalism bind, but a relationship with God brings liberty! God is not a cop who is merely interested in everyone doing right. He is a Father, who longs for the hearts of His children to be turned towards Him, healed by Him, restored through Him, and free in Him. He desires relationship.

Galatians 3:21, 22 says, *Is there a conflict, then, between God's law and God's promises? Absolutely not! If the law cold give us new life, we could be made right with God by obeying it. But the Scriptures declare that we are all prisoners of sin, so we receive God's promise of freedom only by believing in Jesus Christ.*

Freedom does not come by trying hard to achieve it; it comes through Jesus Christ. Remember, the way we view God will determine how we come to Him, and ultimately determine how we live our lives. Begin to pray for a clearer understanding. If we will read and study the Word of God, we can get to know God for who He really is.

Hopefully as you have read these last few chapters, you have been able to identify your own problem areas. Now that you can pinpoint what weighs you down, let's begin to look at the steps needed to overcome them!

Let's Pray:

Father, I know there have been times that I have viewed You through my hurt, confusion, and lack of knowledge, and I have used that view to shape the way I've understood You. I don't want to do that any longer! Please continue to reveal Yourself to me. Help me to walk in the knowledge of who You really are! Let my mind not stand in the way of my freedom! I choose to trust what Your word says to be true. I believe You paid the price for my freedom, and I believe You are good! Continue to show me, Father, the areas in my thinking that don't line up with Your word. Thank You for Your grace, patience, love, and freedom!

Chapter 5 Reflection

Describe your view of God?

_____

_____

_____

_____

_____

How has that view shaped that way you live your life? How has that shaped the way you approach Him?

_____

_____

_____

_____

_____

Is your perspective of God in line with what the Bible says to be true about His nature?_____

_____

_____

_____

_____

Do you often compare yourself to others? How has that robbed you of freedom?

_____

_____

_____

_____

_____

What has your definition of freedom been? Do you see it as just getting to do whatever you want? Does it line up with the Word of God?

_____

_____

_____

_____

Section 2

Losing the Weight

CHAPTER 6

The Power of Peace & Joy

*I*n the 2010 version of the movie, *Karate Kid*, Mr. Han tells Dre, "Being still and doing nothing are two very different things." True indeed!

Psalm 46:10 says, *Be still, and know that I am God.* One thing I am not often good at is being still. Probably like many of you, I can always find something that needs to be done, people to talk to, someone to help, clothes to fold, household jobs to do, errands to run. This command can be very hard to live out, especially when I feel the need to try to control my situations. Let's be honest, we women feel that way a lot. We grasp and strive for different things in life, yet instead of finding freedom in that control; we are burdened and stressed by it.

When life gets hectic we *need* to be still and remember that we are God's daughters. Our circumstances may be overwhelming, our emotions may be all over the place, the future may seem unclear or frightening, or we may have a million things we feel like talking to God about. Those are the moments where, more than anything else, we just need to come to Him, sit in His presence, let Him refresh us and remind us that He is in control, and just *be* His daughters. When we're able to do that, all the chaos gets quieted. We are able to remember who we are, and W*hose* we are. Even if we don't walk away with all the answers, we receive the grace and strength to keep walking!

Peace and joy are very powerful tools, yet many times we overlook them. They either seem too simple or too unattainable amidst our busy lives.

Psalm 34:12 & 14 (NIV) says, *Whoever of you loves life, and desires to see many good days, turn from evil and do good; Seek peace and pursue it.* The Bible actually tells us to *pursue* peace so that in doing so, we gain a good life. Therefore, peace isn't something we just wait to feel; we must go after it.

Nehemiah 8:10 says *"The joy of the Lord is your strength."* I love that verse. Joy isn't some pansy emotion!

It doesn't involve pasting a smile on our faces while inside we're miserable. Best of all, it isn't something we have to fake or muster up on our own. **The joy of the Lord is a tool that enables us to be strong and consistent regardless of our circumstances.**

Psalm 16:11 (NKJV) says, *You will show me the path of life; In Your presence is fullness of joy; At Your right hand are pleasures forevermore.* We find joy by spending time in God's presence. He gives us joy, which becomes our strength, and that strength will carry us through! Thank God we don't have to figure out how to come up with it ourselves! His word tells us where to find it.

Grace for the Moment

Trusting God to meet us in our moment of need isn't an easy way to live. Most of us feel more effective when we worry, stress, and try to control our situations, but how many times does that actually help?

Matthew 6:25-34 says, *That is why I tell you not to worry about everyday life—whether you have enough food and drink, or enough clothes to wear. Isn't life more than food, and your body more than clothing? Look at the birds. They don't plant or harvest or store food in barns, for your heavenly Father feeds them. And aren't you far more valu-able to him than they are? Can all your worries add a single moment to your life? And why worry about your clothing? Look at the lilies of the field and how they grow. They don't work or make their clothing, yet Solomon in all his glory was not dressed as beautifully as they are. And if God cares so wonderfully for wildflowers that are here today and thrown into the fire tomorrow, he will certainly care for you. Why do you have so little faith? So don't worry about these things, saying, 'What will we eat? What will we drink? What will we wear?' These things dominate the thoughts of unbelievers, but your heavenly Father already knows all your needs. Seek the Kingdom of God above all else, and live righteously, and he will give you everything you need. So don't worry about tomorrow, for tomorrow will bring its own worries. Today's trouble is enough for today.*

When we stress out about our circumstances, we are robbed of peace, joy, and freedom. The last verse in the Matthew 6 passage says, *"Today's trouble is enough for today."* Part of losing the negative spiritual weight and living in the freedom of peace and joy, is realizing that God usually gives us **grace for the *moment*.** We want more. We ask for more. We expect more and often get frustrated or disappointed when we don't get what we want when we want it, but we can be sure that when we need God, He is there.

2 Corinthians 12:8-10 (NKJV) says, *Concerning this thing I pleaded with the Lord three times that it might depart from me. And He said to me, 'My grace is* **sufficient** *for you, for My strength is made perfect in weakness.' Therefore most gladly I will rather boast in my infirmities, that the power of Christ may rest upon me. Therefore I take pleasure in infirmities, in reproaches, in needs, in persecutions, in distresses, for Christ's sake. For when I am weak, then I am strong.*

Sufficient means, "adequate for the purpose; enough." God's grace is enough for whatever it is we are going through at that moment. It is *adequate* for our circumstances. Adequate means, "as much or as good as necessary for some requirement or purpose; fully sufficient, suitable, or fit."

We become anxious because we don't want *adequate* grace, we want so much more. In stressful moments and hard times, it would be nice to draw from a "grace file" and know that everything is going to go smoothly. But God gives us grace for the *moment!* He promises to supply our needs, but His timing isn't always what we would choose.

We just need to *remember that* in the moments where we find ourselves overwhelmed and stressed out. God will give us the grace and strength we need to make it through. That truth will help us hold onto our peace and walk in joy.

Trusting God

Trusting God is what allows us to relax, walk in freedom, and *be still* instead of freaking out! Proverbs 3:5-6 says, *Trust in the LORD with all your heart, do not depend on your own understanding. Seek his will in all you do, and he will show you which path to take.* Trusting in the Lord with ALL of our heart leaves no room for our hearts to do their own thing. We have to fully trust, and let God have complete control. Also we need to seek Him in all we do. We *want* God to lead, guide, and direct us, yet we fail to realize that in order for that to happen, we have a part to play, too. God doesn't force us to trust Him or to seek Him. That's all up to us. When we allow doubt, fear, and worry to remain in our lives, we rob ourselves of peace and joy.

The Bible says in James that a double minded man is unstable in all his ways. We can't have both things. We can't have doubt *and* peace operating in our hearts at the same time. God will do His part, but we also must do ours. So if we're going to trust Him, let's trust Him! Let's not just say it with our mouths, and live in doubt with our actions. If we truly desire to live in freedom, we have to be willing to *daily* lay down our urge to control and our need to know and understand everything all the time. After all, that's what trust is all about.

Our Stabilizing Force

Philippians 4:7 says, *Then you will experience God's peace, which exceeds anything we can understand. His peace will guard your hearts and minds as you live in Christ Jesus.*

This is an amazing verse. The Amplified Bible says it like this, *"And God's peace* [shall be yours, that tranquil state of a soul assured of its salvation through Christ, and so fearing nothing from God and being content with its earthly lot of whatever sort that is, that peace] *which transcends all understanding shall garrison and mount guard over your hearts and minds in Christ Jesus."*

The word "garrison" is a military term, and it refers to soldiers being stationed at a certain post to fortify it. God is saying that He will station His peace at the post of our hearts and minds, the two areas where we are most vulnerable! Do we really realize that as Christians we have access to this kind of peace? It's a *calm assurance* that brings stability to our hearts and minds. Even when we don't understand our situations or how they will turn out, we can have peace.

Ephesians 6:15 says, *For shoes, put on the peace that comes from the Good News so that you will be fully prepared.* How many of us have ever tried to squeeze our feet into shoes that didn't quite fit just because we liked them? I know I have, but I also know I never get very far in shoes like that. If we're going to walk, run, exercise, stand, or do anything besides sit, what we put on our feet is very important! The wrong shoes can throw us off balance, whereas the right ones will bring stability, equipping us to run our race.

When I was about seven years old, I had a pair of yellow tennis shoes that I absolutely loved. I also loved to run, and for some reason I believed that those yellow shoes made me run fast. I wore them all the time. Wherever I was going, I wanted those shoes on my feet. They eventually developed a hole in them from being worn so much. I remember the day those sneakers were thrown out. I cried so hard because I thought I would never be able to run fast again! Even in my somewhat lopsided seven-year-old logic, I realized that what was on my feet made a difference.

Ephesians 6 tells us to wear the shoes of peace. **Peace is part of the *armor* of God!** When we are facing battles and hard times, God says one of our weapons is peace! That peace comes from God's Word, enabling us to be prepared for whatever we may face. The more we understand the power of God's peace and joy, the more we can walk in freedom. It goes back to Psalm 46:10. Walking in peace and joy allows us to "be still" in the midst of turmoil. It isn't that we are doing *nothing*! We are allowing God to work in and through our circumstances and us because we choose to walk according to His Word. His peace gives us the calm assurance to face whatever life brings our way, and His joy gives us the strength to keep walking.

The Bible says peace is found in knowing His Word and His promises, and joy comes from spending time in His presence. Hopefully, we will never again look at peace and joy as just simply emotions! They are God-given tools to help us live in freedom rather than the weight of worry and stress. Then we are truly able to live the life God has for us instead of the one we throw together by ourselves.

Romans 15:13 says, *I pray that God, the source of hope, will fill you completely with joy and peace because you trust in him. Then you will overflow with confident hope through the power of the Holy Spirit.*

She's Living Freedom

I've had the opportunity recently to get to know an amazing lady in my church with an incredible story. Jill writes,

"Have you ever been faced with a really bad report? For me it was February 2009. I found myself in the ER, waiting for emergency surgery to stop the hemorrhaging. I had lost more than one half of my blood and could have easily slipped into eternity. But God! I was the woman with the issue of blood and oh how I needed to touch the hem of His garment! Thankfully, my husband and others were there with me, praying for a miracle! I felt the Lord remind me, in the midst of it all, that I still had an assignment and purpose and she was waiting at home for her mama's safe return.

We had prayed and believed God for eleven years for our precious daughter who was only three years old at that time. Even though the diagnosis would be cervical cancer, I knew that nothing would stop the plan of God in my life! After I was released to go home, Psalm 91 (MSG) became my hiding place. *'God, You're my refuge. I trust in You and I'm safe. Fear nothing-Not disease that prowls through the darkness. I'll rescue you, then throw you a party and give you a long life, a long drink of salvation!'* Wow, it was in these promises that I found a peace and joy that went beyond all of my understanding, even in the midst of a storm!

In between my two surgeries, I was watching a well-known evangelist on television pray for a woman. He declared to her that because she knew Jesus as her Lord and Savior, her sickness had to go because it was illegal. I immediately placed my hands on my abdomen and commanded whatever was causing the issue of blood to leave in the name of Jesus because it too was illegal. At that exact moment, I literally felt something like a bird spring from my abdomen and leave! A few days later I had a hysterectomy and the pathology report showed that two of my lymph nodes tested were microscopically tainted. I knew the enemy had only left his footprint. Not long after I picked up my Bible, and read a verse that I had never seen before. *"Like a fluttering sparrow or a darting swallow, an undeserved (illegal) curse does not come to rest."* Proverbs 26:2 (NIV) My heart leaped with joy because I knew God was speaking. The undeserved curse had come, but it did not have the authority to stay! It left like a small bird fluttering away at the name of Jesus!

Later that day, I asked my husband to look up a website that a friend had recommended to me. As soon as he found it he asked me to guess what scripture they had posted on their front page, and I answered Proverbs 26:2! Again, I felt the peace and joy of God's presence sweep over me like a river. I drew comfort and strength in knowing that my Father in Heaven was so mindful of me. When I saw my doctor again he suggested I would need eight to nine chemo treatments, but he would leave that decision up to the radiologist. I prayed that God would give His wisdom to the radiologist and he prescribed five treatments instead. I was so overwhelmed with gratitude! The next day while sharing the good news with a friend, the Lord gave her a word that it would only be four treatments. In the end it *was* only four chemo treatments! I stand today cancer-free, thanking my Heavenly Father for what He has brought me through! I will believe the report of the Lord!'"

She's Living Freedom (Too)

Krista and I have been friends for about nine years. We live in different states now, but she's one of those friends that anytime we're together we pick right back up where we left off. She writes,

"I wouldn't normally put the words *transition, peace,* and *joy,* in the same sentence. They don't naturally exist in the world together. But with God 'naturally' is not always the way He works. I grew up in a pastor's home, and later went in to full-time ministry myself. To say my life has been busy would be an understatement. I have the type of personality that is not fulfilled unless I am involved in everything. I love to lead, serve, create, and motivate others to do the same. Over the past year, my life has taken a dramatic shift. While driving down the road one day I felt the Lord speak to me that it was time for me to have a baby. My husband and I had been married for ten years, but with our hectic ministry schedules we had never taken the time to start a family. I became pregnant very quickly, and although I was excited for this new addition, I also knew it would be a big change for our family.

As the arrival of our precious daughter drew closer, I began to find myself very fearful of the future. What was going to happen? How was it going to happen? When was it going to happen? Being the control freak that I am, I wanted God to lay out His plan for this next season of our lives in perfect detail. Of course, that didn't happen and what did happen was something I could have never seen coming. Just a couple weeks before I was supposed to deliver, God spoke to my husband that it was time to move on from the position we were serving in. After much prayer and confirmation, he put in his resignation. Coincidentally, that just happened to be the day I went into labor! Here I was not only becoming a mom for the first time, but our whole world, as we knew it was being turned upside down. I was filled with questions, doubt, and insecurity about the future. I remember sitting in the hospital room at 3 a.m. rocking my baby, listening to worship music, and crying out to God for something to hold onto.

In that moment with tears streaming down my face I heard the Lord's voice so strongly speak to my heart, 'The best is yet to come.'

In the midst of the biggest transition we had ever faced, I immediately felt such peace and joy. I had no idea what the next step was going to be, but I knew God was in control. He has yet to reveal what the next step is for us, and I would be lying if I said this hasn't been the most difficult season of trusting God I have ever faced. But when I begin to feel my peace slipping away and doubt and fear creeping in again, I go back to that night in the hospital and hold tight to the promise that God spoke so clearly. I don't know what, where, or when, but I know the best is yet come! Numbers 23:19 (NIV) says, *'God is not human, that He should lie, not a human being, that He should change His mind. Does He speak and then not act? Does He promise and not fulfill?'* My peace comes from knowing the character of God, and trusting that in every situation He is working it out for our good."

Let's Pray:

Thank you Father for revealing more of Yourself to me again. Help me to remember that all I have to do is come before You and spend time with You to get refreshed and strengthened. Thank You that You have equipped me with the tools I need to live a life of freedom. Help me to remember Your promises in the midst of hectic days and situations beyond my control. I love being your daughter! Continue to lead and guide me through this time, Father. I won't give in to worry and stress; I will trust and wait on You. Thank You for the refreshment that Your peace and joy bring.

Chapter 6 Reflection

How have you understood peace and joy in the past? Have you seen them as *tools*?

_____

_____

_____

When was the last time you relinquished control to God and actually left it in His hands?

_____

_____

_____

What would pursuing peace look like for you?

_____

_____

_____

Take a moment (and a deep breath) as you pray and allow God's Spirit to wash over you.

CHAPTER 7

Strut Your Stuff

I have three sons, and another one on the way, so I've had the "pleasure" three times now of having to get rid of baby weight! Come this summer, I'll be walking down that road again. With my first son, losing the weight wasn't too difficult. Then I got pregnant again. The second time around wasn't quite as easy as the first. Nursing wasn't enough like it had been with my oldest; I actually had to exercise! The third time around, as many women can attest to after subsequent pregnancies, was the hardest. One morning, I was nursing my son, who was only a few weeks old, when my three-year-old crawled up on the bed with me. He looked down at my stomach, which was still carrying extra weight and wrinkly skin from my stretch marks, and said, "Yuck!

What's that?" Leave it to a child to be so honest. Needless to say, I didn't strut my stuff that day!

Have you ever noticed that when you lose even a few pounds, you tend to walk and dress differently? You pull out the "skinny" jeans or the dress you haven't worn in months. Your step becomes a little bolder, more purposeful. You get a little "strut" going on. It's as if you've not only lost something, but you've also gained something as well.

That is what happens in the natural realm, and it mirrors what takes place in the spiritual realm. When we are able to start getting rid of whatever our problem areas are we begin to live differently! The difference in the natural *and* the spiritual realm is usually confidence. Confidence and freedom go hand in hand. Confident people live differently than insecure people.

One morning the Holy Spirit spoke to me and said, "True confidence has nothing to do with you." I sat there for a minute and then quickly grabbed a piece of paper and pen and wrote that down. Think about that for a minute. True confidence has *nothing* to do with you!

The problem is that many of us think of confidence as a feeling. If we like what we're wearing or how our hair looks we *feel* secure that day. If we've been promoted, or received a compliment, gift, or any other sort of affirmation, it's easy to *feel* good for a time. However, what about when none of those things go our way? How do we act when we don't feel good in what we're wearing, we don't like the way we look, or when no one talks to us or seems to notice anything we've done? We can still *be* confident even when we *feel* insecure.

Let's go back to that statement the Holy Spirit spoke to me. True confidence has nothing to do with us. That really is the theme throughout the Word of God. Let's look at a few verses. I've added my emphasis to the parts of the verse that confirm that statement.

In John 15:5 Jesus says, *Yes, I am the vine; you are the branches. Those who remain in me, and I in them, will produce much fruit. For **apart from me you can do nothing**.*

Luke 1:37 says, *For **with God** nothing will be impossible.*

Philippians 4:13 says, *I can do everything **through Christ, who gives me strength**.*

Romans 8:37 says, *No, despite all these things, overwhelming victory is ours **through Christ** who loved us."*

Ephesians 3:20 (NKJV) says, *"Now to him who is able to do immea-surably more than all we ask or imagine, according to **his power** that is at work within us."*

Joshua 1:9 says, *"This is my command—be strong and coura-geous! Do not be afraid or discouraged. **For the Lord your God is with you** wherever you go.*

See the pattern? Time and time again, God reaffirms who we are and what we can do if we are linked to Him. We can do these things because *He* enables us to. *He* gives us the strength, assurance, and victory. **Confidence has nothing to do with security in ourselves; it has everything to do with our security in God!** It's realizing that we can do nothing truly significant in our own strength but also knowing that *with God* nothing is impossible. How freeing is that? *God's* ability is something I can rest assure in! As I do, I realize that His Spirit at work in my spirit will enable me. Developing true confidence simply comes by shifting our perspective.

We also can't let the phrase "self-confidence" fool us. In our society self-confidence is *all* about what we can do, how we look, what we're wearing, and how we measure up. Self-help books, tapes, and seminars are everywhere. No one wants to live an insecure life. **However, none of those things will truly fix the problem because if they don't involve Christ, then there never is true change!** You can tell me all day long to *believe in myself*, but I know my weaknesses and shortcomings. I know what I can and can't do. I know that I'm human and I'm always going to fall short if I have to figure everything out in my own understanding. So if my security derives from just believing in myself, that's pretty depressing! Thankfully, God offers us a different option than the world does. *True* confidence comes from believing in what God says He can do in and through us!

Only a Facade

My husband likes to unwind by watching sports, so ESPN is on a lot around our household. If you've ever watched ESPN for any amount of time, you notice that they repeat things, so I'll pick up on different names or teams, because I'm hearing them so often. I love the look of surprise my husband gets when I actually know who's on what team and the name of different coaches! Well, in the past few years, several athletes have been caught using steroids. Before those athletes got caught, even the day before, they were still at the top of their game in everyone's eyes. They seemed so self-assured and talented. People talked about how great they were and looked up to them. However, once the steroid use was out in the open, the same people began to question if that athlete *ever* was able to do any of those things on their own. The whole image the person portrayed was shattered. As the facade slipped away, the truth was revealed.

I really believe that's like the confidence many people possess today. It's a false front, and if we were able to look inside, we wouldn't see security at all. Rather, we would see fear that has been carefully covered up. Confidence isn't about mustering up a certain ability or appearance. It's not about putting on a tough face and attitude that says "I don't need anyone, and no one can hurt me." It's not about being Miss or Mrs. Independent. That way of thinking is false and damaging, but it's exactly what our society portrays as desirable. As women of God, let's pull that facade down!

When our assurance is in ourselves, we are secure only as long as we are achieving and have our lives well put together. When those things get disturbed, so does our positive self-image. When our certainty is in God, however, we are secure no matter what our situation looks like. We rest in the knowledge that *He* is able, *He* is perfect, and *He* never fails. He is our Source, and that Source is limitless! That knowledge brings confidence.

It's Okay to Strut

Hebrews 10:35 (NIV) says, *So do not throw away your confidence; it will be richly rewarded.* We can't throw away what we don't have. We might feel we don't have confidence, but as children of God we do. The Spirit of the Most High lives inside of us, and as we talked about in Chapter 2, He *is* confident! We possess His assurance; we just might not walk in it *yet.* God has given all of us gifts, abilities, and talents, and we're not being prideful to acknowledge those things. God gives us His blessings for a reason and wants us to use them.

Romans 12:6-8 says, *In his grace, God has given us different gifts for doing certain things well. So if God has given you the ability to prophesy, speak out with as much faith as God has given you. If your gift is serving others, serve them well. If you are a teacher, teach well. If your gift is to encourage others, be encouraging. If it is giving, give generously. If God has given you leadership ability, take the responsibility seriously. And if you have a gift for showing kindness to others, do it gladly.*

1 Peter 4:10-11 says, *God has given each of you a gift from his great variety of spiritual gifts. Use them well to serve one another. Do you have the gift of speaking? Then speak as though God himself were speaking through you. Do you have the gift of helping others? Do it with all the strength and energy that God supplies. Then everything you do will bring glory to God through Jesus Christ. All glory and power to him forever and ever! Amen.*

If we don't acknowledge and walk in the things God has given us, we can't be effective for His kingdom! We are usually much quicker to point out our weaknesses than our strengths. Either we feel a sense of false humility by diminishing the strengths God has given us, we're too afraid to acknowledge them, or we just don't look for them. But here's the thing. God does not get glory from us living insecure lives! His presence is not seen in us when we are holding back or hiding. Being confident in what God is doing in us is not prideful. **God is glorified, people are blessed, and we are fulfilled when we are walking, with purpose, in the things He has called us to do!**

I love Psalm 139: 13-16 which says, *"Oh yes, you shaped me first inside, then out; you formed me in my mother's womb. I thank you, High God—you're breathtaking! Body and soul, I am marvelously made! I worship in adoration—what a creation! You know me inside and out, you know every bone in my body; you know exactly how I was made, bit by bit, how I was sculpted from nothing into something. Like an open book, you watched me grow from conception to birth;" all the stages of my life were spread out before you, The days of my life all prepared before I'd even lived one day.*" (The Message)

Do we worship God for how He made us? The verse says, *"Body and soul, I am marvelously made! I worship in adoration-what a creation!"* That's a bold statement and often hard to say about ourselves. However the more we realize that God offers us a confidence that goes beyond what we see or feel, the easier it becomes to embrace it.

So strut your stuff with a smile on your face! And by the way, it's not a strut that makes others feel bad. In fact, it's one that offers hope and pulls them along too!

Let's Pray:

Father, thank You for the confidence that You have instilled inside of me. Thank You that Your Spirit enables me and equips me. I know that on my own I always come up short, but thank You that with You NOTHING is impossible! Continue to help me remember that. I will choose to walk in confidence and not insecurity, because I know that You have created me to be an overcomer!

Chapter 7 Reflection

How do you feel about the statement "true confidence has nothing to do with you"?

_____

_____

_____

Do you consider yourself confident? Why? Or Why Not?

_____

_____

_____

What are the things that make you feel confident? Do those things line up with what the Word of God says to be true?

_____

_____

_____

Take a moment and determine to allow God's Word to be the basis of your security.

Chapter 8

Living Loved

❧

*R*emember sitting as a little girl with a daisy in your hand, picking off the petals one by one saying, "He loves me, he loves me not"? I do; in fact, my friends and I would try to rig our flowers so that we'd always end up with "He loves me" in the end. Even from the time we were children, we've all had the same desire we have as adults. We long to know that we are loved. That yearning is woven into the depths of our hearts. God created us with it, not so that we'd find another person to meet that need, but so that He could. He wants to be the One to lavish His love on us.

As little girls we allowed the flower petals to jokingly determine whether we were loved or not. As adults, we often allow our circumstances to determine God's love for us. Unfortunately, it's not cute and funny like the flower petals were. In fact, that mentality is very damaging. If we don't understand God's love as it is stated in His word, then we find ourselves on a roller coaster of feeling loved when things are good, and feeling forgotten by God when they aren't. This mindset simply isn't the truth.

God loves us passionately and whole-heartedly. If you have grown up in church, you have most likely heard that many times. Even if you haven't been to church a day in your life, you probably have still heard someone talk about God's love.

So then why is it that so few of us really live in it? Why is it easier for us to think that God is always mad at us, rather than to think about His love for us? I've been a Christian for many years now, and I still find myself asking God sometimes if He's mad at me. That usually happens when I can't feel His presence, or I haven't heard Him speak to my heart, or when things are chaotic in my life.

One morning I was feeling this way, so I put on worship music and started praying, as I was getting ready for the day. I was in a season of life where I hadn't been *feeling* a whole lot. Why do we base so much on feelings anyway? I had two toddlers at home and was pregnant with our third son, so I wasn't always getting the time I would have liked to be with the Lord. On that morning, however, I heard the Holy Spirit telling me how much God loved me.

I found myself wondering why it's so hard to believe His love over the idea that He must be mad at me about something. I felt the Lord remind me of Romans 8:38-39, *"And I am convinced that nothing can ever separate us from God's love. Neither death nor life, neither angels nor demons, neither our fears for today nor our worries about tomorrow—not even the powers of hell can separate us from God's love. No power in the sky above or in the earth below—indeed, nothing in all creation will ever be able to separate us from the love of God that is revealed in Christ Jesus our Lord."*

I've read that verse before but never taken it into the depths of my heart. NOTHING can take away God's love for us! He isn't mad at us. Throughout Scripture, we find a God who is passionate about His people, *even when* they turn their backs on Him. Remember the Israelites we talked about in Chapter 5? No matter what they did, God took them back and blessed them every time they repented. He restored them and gave them incredible favor. He does the same for us. No matter what we do or have ever done, God is not mad at us! He is standing by our side waiting for us to come to

Him. He is waiting for us to realize, believe, and walk in the truth about His love.

God created us, and His love for us is unconditional. We hear that word associated with the love of God, but let's look at the definition for a better understanding. The word unconditional means, "Limited by no conditions, absolute." There are NO conditions to God's love. Think about it for a minute. That means we don't have to do anything to earn it. That's refreshing! God wholeheartedly loves us. He is interested in who we are, not just in what we can do. He loves us with our good and our bad, our strengths and our weaknesses. We don't have to be perfect. In fact, we were never meant to be perfect, or to try to act like we are, thank God! There is no need to because God sees everything about us and loves us with all His heart. His love does not change. It does not waiver. It will not go away.

Actually living like we are loved is so freeing! What relationships do you have where you just know you are completely loved, and you are confident in that love? For me, it's my relationship with my husband. For some, it may also be a spouse, or a friend, a parent, a sister, or other family member. For most of us, we don't have *very many* of those relationships.

I know Aryan loves me. I'm confident of that love. He tells me, he shows me, and I can see and feel it. In our day-to-day life, I don't feel the need to try to earn his love. In our conversations, I don't feel like I have to say all the right things to earn his approval. If I want to ask him something, I don't first go through a series of motions or phrases to build up to it. I just talk to him. Even when I don't say all the right things, even when in my anger or frustration I snap at him or say something I regret, I know that I can apologize and we will make it right.

Stay with me here, because I'm not giving an excuse to be rude in our relationships. I just want to drive home a point. I don't worry that our relationship is going to be over every time we disagree about something, because I know that we love each other. I am loved in my marriage, and that knowledge brings freedom. I don't have to perform for him; I can just *be* with him.

Because I'm secure and confident in our love, I *want* to do things that please him. I want to make sure he is happy and feels taken care of. I *want* to please him because I love him, and I know he loves me. I don't *try* to please him because I'm scared that if I don't, he won't love me. See the difference?

127

Which way do you view your relationship with God? The actions outwardly might look similar, but the state of our hearts is where the difference will be. Knowing we're loved brings freedom. Feeling the need to earn love is burdensome, and in time will hinder a relationship. God wants us to know we are loved so we can be secure and confident in our relationship with Him.

Why it's Hard to Believe

The enemy knows the freedom that we will have when we truly learn to believe and live in the love God has for us, so he sows deception into our hearts whenever he can. John 8:44 says this about the devil, *"He has always hated the truth, because there is no truth in him. When he lies, it is consistent with his character; for he is a liar and the father of lies."*

He will do whatever it takes to keep us from believing God's love. Revelation 12:10 refers to Satan as *"the accuser of the brethren,"* and that is exactly what he does. He brings to our minds every reason why God couldn't possibly love us the way He does, and he makes his accusations sound so convincing. He throws every sin, weakness, and insecurity in our faces to keep our heads down and our spirits dry. That is called condemnation!

To condemn, according to the *World English Dictionary*, is "to express strong disapproval of" or "to judge or pronounce unfit for use." Those are precisely the feelings the enemy wants to project onto us. He wants us to believe that God disapproves of us and considers us unfit to love. It's very important that we realize where these feelings come from. They do not come from God! Romans 8:1 says, *So now there is no condemnation for those who belong to Christ Jesus.* When we find ourselves feeling those emotions of condemnation, we need to realize the enemy is trying to rob us of the freedom that comes from living in the love of God.

What the Bible says

1 John 3:1 (NIV) says, *See what great love the Father has lavished on us, that we should be called children of God! And that is what we are!* Long ago the Lord said to Israel: *"I have loved you, my people, with an everlasting love. With unfailing love I have drawn you to myself."* Jeremiah 31:3

In the New King James Version of the Bible the word love is mentioned 494 times. The word anger is only mentioned 230 times. The amount of times love is mentioned more than doubles the amount of times anger is, yet we are so quick to think of God as being mad at us! In fact, so many Scriptures throughout the Bible refer to God as being *slow* to anger or turning away His anger. Let's look at some of them:

Nehemiah 9:17 says, *They refused to obey, and did not remember the miracles you had done for them. Instead, they became stubborn and appointed a leader to take them back to their slavery in Egypt! But you are a God of forgiveness, gracious and merciful, slow to become angry, and rich in unfailing love. You did not abandon them.*

Psalm 30:5 says, *For His anger lasts only a moment, but His favor lasts a lifetime; weeping may last for the night, but joy comes with the morning.*

Psalm 78:37-39 (NKJV) says, *For their heart was not steadfast with Him, nor were they faithful in His covenant. But He, being full of compassion, forgave their iniquity, and did not destroy them. Yes, many a time He turned His anger away, and did not stir up all His wrath; for He remembered that they were but flesh, a breath that passes away and does not come again.*

Psalm 145:8 (NKJV) says, *The Lord is gracious and full of compassion, slow to anger and great in mercy.*

Joel 2:13 (NKJV) says, *So rend your heart, and not your garments; return to the LORD your God, for He is gracious and merciful, slow to anger, and of great kindness; and He relents from doing harm.*

Micah 7:18 (NKJV) says, *Who is a God like You, pardoning iniquity and passing over the transgression of the remnant of His heritage? He does not retain His anger forever, because He delights in mercy.*

We typically view God as being quick to get mad at us when we fall short, but His Word says otherwise. He is our Father and loves us very much. Some of us haven't had the greatest example of an earthly father, so we find it hard to relate to the goodness of our Heavenly Father. But if we will allow Him to, God will begin to make Himself known to us, and we will see His love in many ways. He didn't save us and call us to Himself so He could show us how mad He is at us. He did it so we could experience His infinite love both now and in eternity!

1 Thessalonians 5:8-10 says, *But let us who live in the light be clearheaded, protected by the armor of faith and love, and wearing as our helmet the confidence of our salvation. For God chose to save us through our Lord Jesus Christ, not to pour out His anger on us. Christ died for us so that, whether we are dead or alive when He returns, we can live with Him forever.* Allow that verse into the depths of your heart!

The Difference

Research shows that babies and children thrive on love. When children are raised in a loving environment, they develop better mentally, physically, and emotionally, and are more secure in their day-to-day lives. Studies have shown that the brain actually develops better in babies who are given love. Children who do not receive love in the first year of life are at risk for emotional and physical problems as they grow up.

Common knowledge is that, as individuals, we live differently when we know we are loved. We are more secure and less likely to be weighed down by depression, fear, insecurity, stress, disappointment, and bitterness. We are able to enjoy our lives! Even as adults, we thrive on love. We can look around and see that many of the hurting people we know or pass by do not experience love in their daily lives. But here's the thing. As children of God, regardless of what we may experience in our earthly relationships, we are always loved by our Heavenly Father! We can be secure in that love, because it's more than a feeling; it's a fact. We are loved! But if we don't live in that love, we don't experience the freedom it brings.

In Matthew 23:37, Jesus is talking to the people in the city of Jerusalem, His chosen people, and He says, *"How often I wanted to gather your children together, as a hen gathers her chicks under her wings, but you were not willing!"* God extends His love to us as His children, but we have to accept it, believe it, and live in it. Remember John 10:10? Jesus came so we can have and live an abundant life. The more we realize how much God loves us, the more we can live that kind of life.

More Than Head Knowledge

The proof of God's love is throughout His word, but we have to read it to know it. Once we know His truths, we have to begin to walk in them. It's not enough to *know* God's love exits. If we want change to occur in our lives, if we want to live in freedom, we must *live* like we are loved. We can't

133

go around thinking God is always mad or disappointed in us. Recognize the accusing voice of the enemy and know it isn't God's. Let's speak His word over our lives! If you are having a hard time believing it, put Scriptures about His love on your wall, mirror, dashboard, refrigerator, and get them into your spirit! His Word renews our minds.

Shed the weight that condemnation brings and live in the freedom that comes from knowing you are loved! Remember *nothing* can separate us from His love. It's real, and it's not too good to be true. It is wonderful, amazing, and good. Yet it *is* true!

Let's Pray:

Father, Your love is incredible! I find it hard to believe sometimes that You love me so much, but I'm learning to trust and walk in it. Thank You that You never give up on me. Thank You for Your patience and Your willingness to love me despite my mistakes and imperfections. There are times I wish I could physically feel Your arms around me, but I know that You never leave me or forsake me, and You surround me with Your love. I know it is more than a feeling. Help me to live each day secure and confident in the infinite love that You have poured upon me as Your child!

Chapter 8 Reflection

Do you find the knowledge of God's love for you hard or easy to believe? Why is that?

_____

_____

_____

What relationship do you have where you know that you are loved regardless? Are you that person for anyone else?

_____

_____

_____

Have you ever felt like God's love wasn't for you? What made you feel that way?

_____

_____

_____

Read Romans 8:38-39 again and let the Holy Spirit remind you right now of how true those verses are.

Section 3

Keeping It Off!

CHAPTER 9

Daily Choices

———— ❦ ————

O ne day early in our marriage, on our day off, I
convinced my husband to go climb one of our local
mountains. The morning was beautiful, and I was feeling
excited! The mountain looked bigger to me standing at the
bottom than I had realized, but I felt energized as we started
heading up. We had made it about a third of the way, when
my legs started burning and my excitement wore off. I suggested to my husband that we could go halfway that day,
and come back another time. But he *lovingly* let me know
that I hadn't dragged him out of bed so early on his day off
to climb halfway. We were going to the top! I realized at
that point that my choice to climb the mountain was one I
was going to have to keep making, every step of the way.
It wasn't enough to decide at the bottom of the mountain

when everything was easy and I was excited. I had to *keep choosing* to climb the whole way up! We finally made it to the top, and the view was definitely worth seeing. I was so glad I hadn't given up when I felt like it.

Freedom is not a one-time choice. It is something that must be worked for and lived out on a daily basis. 2 Corinthians 5:17 says, *This means that anyone who belongs to Christ has become a new person. The old life is gone; a new life has begun!* When we lose weight, there is more than a physical change going on. The body is changing, but we won't keep weight off by making the same poor choices in eating and exercise habits that contributed to weight gain in the first place. The same concept applies spiritually. When we get rid of the things that weigh us down, we must not turn around and pick them up again. As children of God, we are given new life. We don't have to be fearful, insecure, angry, complacent, or bitter any longer. The enemy wants us to hold on to those things, but the choice is ours.

In order to avoid going back to our old ways of thinking and living, we must first understand the concept of change. Romans 12:2 (The Message) says, *So here's what I want you to do, God helping you: Take your everyday, ordinary life-your sleeping, eating, going-to-work, and walking-around life- and place it before God as an offering. Embracing what God does for you is the best thing you can do for him. Don't become so well-adjusted to your culture that you fit into it without even thinking. Instead, fix your attention on God. You'll be changed from the inside out. Readily recognize what he wants from you, and quickly respond to it. Unlike the culture around you, always dragging you down to its level of immaturity, God brings the best out of you, develops well-formed maturity in you.*

In order to *change*, we are actually going to have to *make some changes*! By definition, transformation does not occur unless something different is happening. It requires action on *our* part. We have to make choices that bring these shifts about.

Sowing and Reaping

The practice of sowing and reaping has been around since the earth was created. What is sown will be reaped. If we plant tomato seeds, tomatoes are the result. If we sow pumpkin seeds, we harvest pumpkins. Rose plants yield roses. Galatians 6:7-8 (The Message) says, *Don't be misled: No one makes a fool of God. What a person plants, he will harvest. The person who plants selfishness, ignoring the needs of others—ignoring God!—harvests a crop of weeds. All he'll have to show for his life is weeds! But the one who plants in response to God, letting God's Spirit do the growth work in him, harvests a crop of real life, eternal life.* We get out what we put in. The choices we make now determine how we will live presently and in the future.

What is being sown into your life? Is it positive or negative? Is it in line with the Word of God and the Spirit of God? Are we allowing ourselves to dwell on thoughts of discouragement, doubt, anger, fear, depression, inadequacy, etc? What kinds of things do we speak over ourselves throughout the day? Do we believe what people say about us more than what God says about us? Those are all choices!

If we want a new way of living, we have to change what we are sowing! We must sow good seeds like: Scripture, prayer, praise, and the wise counsel of godly friends who encourage us and speak the truth in love. Those seeds will take root, grow, and bring life and freedom. We need to plant truth and differentiate between it and our feelings. Galatians 6:9 says, *So let's not get tired of doing what is good. At just the right time we will reap a harvest of blessing if we don't give up.* Put God's Word first above your feelings or another's opinion. When we find our acceptance and value in God, we are not as desperate to find it in others.

Let's look again at Philippians 4:13: *For I can do everything through Christ who gives me strength.* Every excuse we can think of is answered right there in that verse. It doesn't say "some" things or "most" things. And remember this is not "in our own strength." The verse says *"everything...through Him."* We don't have to do life alone. So whether we're afraid, tired, weak, doubtful, insecure, etc., the promise is there for us!

Sow seeds of God's promise. You can do it! He will give you the strength.

Victim Mentality

Most people who put on a lot of weight can truthfully pinpoint why it happened. For some people it is depression, divorce, a loss, a breakup or another tragic event. For some people, weight gain is hereditary or stems from the way they were raised. For others, it might be that children, work, and busyness have blocked healthy choices. There are many reasons, but at some point a decision has to be made: continue on the same path or change.

Since this book is not about physical weight loss, we aren't going to investigate those issues in depth. Instead, let's look at how that happens in our spiritual and emotional lives. With God's help, most of us can pinpoint where we picked up the extra "weight." We can link our bitterness or anger to a specific event or multiple events. In the first section of this book, we talked about defining our problem areas and realizing why they are obstacles for us. In order to live free, we have to take responsibility, use the weapons God gives us, and make wise choices rather than continue to carry the weight of our burdens. The Lord says we can give our burdens over to Him. Matthew 11:28-30 says, *Then Jesus said, 'Come to me, all of you who are weary and carry heavy burdens, and I will give you rest. Take my yoke upon you. Let me teach you, because I am humble and gentle at heart, and you will find rest for your souls. For my yoke is easy to bear, and the burden I give you is light.'*

We also can't let our past be used as an **excuse** to keep us bound any longer! I could live my whole life as an insecure mess because my father committed suicide when I was young, or I can *choose* to believe God's Word, accept His healing, and walk in His freedom. One way of life keeps me a victim, but the other way allows me to walk in victory!

I'm not saying that choice is easy (in fact, it's almost always hard), but I am saying it's *my* choice. Certain things may have had a hand in getting us to the state of being weighed down, but no one is forcing us to walk in bondage. If we stay that way, it's because we are choosing to. Regardless of what has happened, in Christ we are no longer victims! **We have the freedom of choice, so let's choose freedom!**

Not Instantly but in an Instant

Weight loss doesn't happen instantly (although I'm sure we all wish it did), neither in the physical nor the spiritual realms. It takes time. The Holy Spirit will renew our minds as we stay in God's Word and dwell on His promises. **The change doesn't happen instantly, but in an instant we do make a choice to either walk in a way that promotes freedom or to pick up the weight that encumbers us.** Whereas we may not get rid of bitterness or anger right away, when those feelings arise, *in that instant* we decide what we are going to do in response. When insecurities threaten to hold us back, *we choose* whether or not they will. Transformation doesn't happen overnight, but it does happen with each decision we make. If you have made several bad choices, start making good ones. One at a time.

Simple Doesn't Mean Easy

As I've studied the Word of God, I've come to realize that His ways are *simple,* but they are usually not *easy*! They require us to get out of our comfort zone, be disciplined, and unselfish. What I mean by "simple" is that His ways are not complicated. In fact, they are quite straightforward. We are the ones who complicate things. When someone wrongs us, we must forgive them. It's simple. Our reaction should not be one we have to wonder about or pray over. God has already commanded us: Forgive. But is that easy? Usually not. The Bible says to *"rejoice in the Lord always"* (Phil. 4:4). *Always*? That is not an easy one either! We are to love people, regardless if they are nice to us. The Bible says that as much as it depends on us, we are to *"live at peace with everyone"* (Rom. 12:18). That's fine for the people we *like* being around, but what about the ones who have offended us? Again, not easy, and in general, we like easy. The hard things we have to work at. But comfortable isn't always beneficial. Each one of our actions and reactions is a choice, and our choices shape our present and our future. Choose God's ways. Let's not complicate our lives with baggage that will weigh us down.

She's Living Freedom

For a short season I had the privilege of working alongside a very energetic, fun-loving woman. Everyone smiles when they are around her. We didn't work together long, but in that time, an ongoing friendship formed that I am so very thankful for. Lena writes,

"Three years ago I was diagnosed with cancer which was one of those blows in life I never thought I'd face. The diagnosis came in the middle of the divorce and child custody battle that I never saw myself going through either. I was a single mom, working full-time, raising two daughters, and going through chemo. There were days I felt so completely drained, and I knew the enemy was attacking the little strength I did have. However, I had made a decision to fight the good fight of faith, and I wasn't going to back down.

Everything I had learned from the Word of God, all the sermons I had listened to, the Bible classes and prayer had equipped me to fight. My trust in who God is gave me the courage to win! Fear, doubt, and hopelessness tried often to overwhelm me, so I had to be resolved at what I was going to choose: life or death, blessings or curses. It was (and is still) a daily choice! I have been cancer-free for three and half years now, praise God! However, living in freedom is still a decision I (we) must make each day. We have the authority and must decide to exercise it. I choose to spend time with the Lord in prayer and worship, speaking the Word over my circumstances each day sometimes several times a day. Faith comes by hearing the Word. We must make the deposits of His Word into our spirits, so in the day of affliction we can make a withdrawal. It is a decision we must make even in the face of fear."

Aha!

In chapter 1, we looked at Galatians 5:1 (NIV), *"It is for freedom that Christ has set us free."*

Now I understand the reason it needs to be explained. I don't wake up everyday and choose to walk in freedom. I need God to remind me every now and then, "Alison, don't walk in your insecurities. Walk in My freedom; it's all yours!" I think Jesus knew we needed that reminder. So walk as He instructs, and when you feel those things that you've let go of start rearing their ugly heads again, speak God's

Word over your life. Remind yourself again how much He loves you. Decide that no matter how you feel, you will *choose* to take God at His word and walk in freedom. When you do, you catch the heart of God. John 8:36 says, *So if the Son sets you free, you are truly free*. That's the bottom line. We have been set free!

Let's Pray:

Thank You Father, that You have given me the ability to make choices. Thank You that Your word is full of guidance for me as I make those choices. Help me to remember that You are leading me, and that all I have to do is ask for Your help when I need it. Help me not to get deterred by the hard choices in life. Please give me the strength and discernment to choose wisely. Father, today I choose freedom. I won't allow the enemy to play mind games with me. I won't give in to my feelings when they are contrary to Your Word. Thank You for the abundant life You have given me. With Your help, I choose to walk in it!

Chapter 9 Reflection

Do your daily choices reflect freedom or bondage?

_____

_____

_____

What do you typically do when faced with hard decisions?

_____

_____

_____

Give an example of how God has given you the strength to choose wisely?

_____

_____

_____

What are some lifestyle changes you need to make in order to live in freedom?

_____

_____

_____

Decide right now to allow the power of the Holy Spirit to help you make those changes and give you His wisdom for daily life.

Chapter 10

Contagious Freedom

————— ⚜ —————

*W*hen a woman finds something good, she can rarely keep it to herself. Whether it's a shoe sale, a great recipe, a good book, or some other amazing discovery, women like to tell others about what they've found. Our spiritual journeys should be the same. Now that we have discovered how incredible true freedom can be, let's not keep it to ourselves!

As I'm closing this book, I have pink eye! My boys have it, too. Anyone with kids knows how contagious (and annoying) pink eye is. Once one person comes into direct contact with the virus, it's easy for everyone else in the household to come down with it, especially when kids are small and they like to touch *everything*! Now, pink eye is never something I want to catch *or* spread, but there are

152

other things in our spiritual lives that are just as contagious. In fact, we catch things from each other all the time!

We have so many opportunities to interact with people throughout our daily lives. Whether at the grocery store, the workplace, a restaurant, the bank, a gas station, the mall, church, or our own homes, we have a sphere of influence around us. Even if our encounters with others are brief, we still have an opportunity to affect them either positively or negatively. Joy can be contagious, but so can a bad attitude. **As daughters of God, we are walking around with the answer that most of the world is still searching for.** Are people catching that from us? When others come into contact with us, is it a refreshing experience or a draining one?

A Beautiful Example

Luke 1:39-45 tells a story about two women who are each carrying a miracle child inside of their wombs. Here is what it says: *"A few days later Mary hurried to the hill country of Judea, to the town where Zechariah lived. She entered the house and greeted Elizabeth. At the sound of Mary's greeting, Elizabeth's child leaped within her, and Elizabeth was filled with the Holy Spirit. Elizabeth gave a glad cry and exclaimed to Mary, "God has blessed you above all women, and your child is blessed. Why am I so honored, that the mother of my Lord should visit me? When I heard your greeting, the baby in my womb jumped for joy. You are blessed because you believed that the Lord would do what he said."*

As Mary simply walks in and says "hello," Elizabeth's baby leaps inside of her, and she is filled with the Holy Spirit. That's quite an entrance! Mary's presence is contagious, and it rubs off on Elizabeth. Joy can be heard in Elizabeth's words as she talks to Mary. Nowhere in that chapter or the ones thereafter does it talk about how Elizabeth even knew Mary was pregnant. An angel told Mary about Elizabeth's pregnancy, but the Bible doesn't record if Elizabeth was told beforehand or if the Holy Spirit revealed it her as He filled her. We don't know that answer, but regardless of how or when Elizabeth realized it, Mary's presence had an *obvious* effect on her cousin.

We should be able to have a similar effect on those with whom we meet. Mary's presence created that reaction because she was carrying Jesus inside of her. You know what? If you have surrendered your life to Christ, then you are too! Mary physically carried Jesus inside of her body, but as God's children, we spiritually carry Him inside of us.

In chapter 2, we looked at Romans 8:11. Let's read the Message translation which says, *"It stands to reason, doesn't it, that if the alive-and-present God who raised Jesus from the dead moves into your life, he'll do the same thing in you that he did in Jesus, bringing you alive to himself? When God lives and breathes in you (and he does, as surely as he did in Jesus), you are delivered from that dead life. With His Spirit living in you, your body will be as alive as Christ's!"* Remember, if we have the Spirit of God inside of us, that life-giving Spirit has changed us, freed us, and given us hope. If you have accepted Christ's offer of salvation, then **the Spirit of God *lives* and *breathes* inside of *you*!** Just like Mary had an effect on Elizabeth, the presence of God inside of us should be contagious to the people with whom we cross paths.

<u>She's Living Freedom (and Passing it On)</u>

Debbie is a spiritual mentor to me and a lady I love and dearly admire. She writes,

"I have been a Christian most of my life and love the Lord with my whole being. However, when it came time to share my faith, I was so afraid. I would pray with people concerning problems in their life, but leading people to Jesus terrified me.

Time passed and I became a nurse. One of my patients had an aggressive form of throat cancer. When I went into her room one night she said to me, 'I'm dying...I hope I'm good enough to make it into Heaven.' On her wall were all her certificates for volunteer work and plaques for foster parenting. Upon hearing her statement, I knew she wasn't ready, but again I was filled with fear. Jesus spoke to my heart and said, 'If you don't do this now, she will spend eternity without Me.' So I followed my heart and began to talk to her. She prayed with me and accepted Jesus Christ as her Savior! A couple days later, she was physically much worse. She was confused, agitated, and yelled at me to 'get out' of her room. I asked her if she remembered me, but she said no. Then I asked her if she remembered praying the other night. Her face cleared, she smiled at me and said, 'That's when I asked Jesus to come into my heart.'

My encounter with that dear lady set me free from my fear! I have since become a Hospice nurse and have had many amazing experiences like this one with several of my patients. I have had the opportunity to lead more than ten people to the Lord. I have also prayed with dozens of patients over the past nine-and-a-half years. I am so thankful I was obedient to the Lord's voice that night. Once I simply put my trust in the Lord and allowed His Spirit inside of me to lead me, I became able to live out a faith that is contagious, offering hope to the people the Lord brings across my path."

What Are People Catching From Us?

Typically, when something is thrown to us we try to catch it, almost instinctively. As children most of us learn how to catch and toss. We may not physically be throwing things, but when others come into contact with us, they are catching something from us! So what are people catching from you? More importantly, what are you "throwing" to them? We give off what we have inside. After reading Romans 8:11, we can't say that we have nothing to give. We are full of great things! We should be spreading the characteristics of God everywhere we go. Colossians 4:6 (NKJV) says, *Let your conversation be always full of grace, seasoned with salt, so that you may know how to answer everyone.* All of us have opportunities to talk with people. The Word of God says that in our conversations our words should be graceful. People should get a taste of the goodness of God when they talk to us. This does not mean that we are to preach a sermon to everyone we talk to, but we are to make the most of our opportunities to be gracious, compassionate, joyful, and kind. Allow the freedom God has given you to rub off on others.

The more we walk in freedom, the more we *want* others to catch it! We begin to look at people differently. Offenses don't stick as easily. We aren't in such a hurry to brush past people. The more we extend freedom to others, the greater capacity we have to walk in it ourselves.

Finish Your Race

We read Hebrews 12:1-3 at the beginning of this book. *Strip down, start running—and never quit! No extra spiritual fat, no parasitic sins. Keep your eyes on Jesus, who both began and finished this race we're in. Study how he did it. Because he never lost sight of where he was headed— that exhilarating finish in and with God.* (The Message) Hopefully, you have begun stripping off that excess weight of burdens, sins, and/or inadequacies layer by layer. As you endeavor to keep up your physical appearance, don't forget that your spirit needs work, too. Keep your eyes on Jesus and *continue* to study how He lived.

Living freedom doesn't happen overnight. It happens *every day* with each choice we make. When you find yourself slipping back into old habits and routines, remind yourself that you've dropped the weight that leads to bondage and you don't need to pick it up again. I pray that you have realized the freedom God has already given you as His daughter, the freedom to be confident, joyful, full of hope, and excited about life! This freedom keeps you *from* worry, fear, unforgiveness, bitterness, offense, insecurity, and every other snare the enemy tries to bring into your life.

You are amazing, daughter of the Most High, and you were created to live an abundant life in close relationship with your Heavenly Father! **You are loved. You have been chosen, provided for, and you carry with you the promise of victory.** Remind yourself of Deuteronomy 30:19-20; you have the choice everyday between life and death, so choose life! Choose freedom! The price has already been paid. It's yours. Live free. And as you do, give freedom away to others who desperately need it.

Let's Pray:

Father, I want to thank You again for the freedom You have given me. Thank You for the sacrifice that Jesus made to purchase it. Thank You for revealing to me the areas that have held me back in the past. Thank You for reminding me of the weapons You have entrusted me with to fight for my freedom. Help me to extend this freedom I have found to those I come into contact with. Help me to be aware of the people you bring across my path. I know that Your Spirit lives inside of me, and therefore I have access to the life-giving power He brings. As others see that in me, let them be drawn to You, so that they can experience it, too! Thank You for transforming my life! I'm in awe of how far You've brought me, and I'm excited to see what's still ahead. I love You.

Chapter 10 Reflection

When you are around others, what do they "catch" from you?

_____

_____

_____

Do you offer the hope of a life of freedom? If not, how can you start?

_____

_____

_____

As you go throughout your day, do you ever stop to think about the life-giving power of God residing in you? How does that affect the way you live?

_____

_____

_____

Take a moment and ask the Holy Spirit to help you spread the freedom He has given you to others.

Endnotes

1. www.dailymail.co.uk/health/article-430913

2. http://quotes.dictionary com/i_hate_to_see_compla cency_prevail_in_our